# en(compass)

## The Poetry Caravan Anthology

Edited by Usha Akella
Foreword by Billy Collins

*To bring poets and poetry to people in our community
who cannot reach poetry on their own.*

**Yuganta Press**

**Editor:** Usha Akella

**Co-Editors:** Brenda Connor-Bey and Sana Mulji Dutt
**Proofreader:** Linda Simone
**Cover Design & Title:** Usha Akella

*en(compass)* is the first anthology of the Poetry Caravan poets, a volunteer organization in White Plains, NY, whose mission is

*to bring poets and poetry to people in our community*
*who cannot reach poetry on their own.*

Poetry workshops and readings are provided to people in senior centers, women's shelters and healthcare facilities—wherever there is the potential for outreach and a chance to make connections. All programs are free to participants. The Poetry Caravan is founded by Poet Usha Akella and was launched as an initiative of the Arts and Culture Committee of the Town of Greenburgh in October 2003. *en(compass)* presents the poetry of the Poetry Caravan's poets and workshops' participants.

**Acknowledgments**
**A Veggie's Valentine** by Jay Albrecht. First appeared in *Let the Poets Speak*, 2002, Arts & Culture Committee, Town of Greenburgh. Reprinted by permission of the author. By Brenda Connor-Bey: **Panama Fishing Man,** first appeared in *Main Trend Magazine, 1981, Main Trend, Inc., NY*. **Alice's Shoes,** first appeared in *Cultural Council Foundation's Spring newsletter, 1980*. Reprinted by permission of the author. **I Met Two Horses** by Michael Carman. Accepted for publication in *Rattapallax*. Published here by permission of Rattapallax. **Nothing is Lost** by Doretta Cornell. First appeared in */Review for Religious/ Quarterly 63.1*. Reprinted by permission of the author. **I stoned the devil, stoned the dream** by Sana Mulji Dutt. First appeared in *existere quarterly, volume 21, issue 2* . Reprinted by permission of the author. By Kathryn Fazio: **The Moving**, first appeared in *Medicinal Purposes Literary Review*. **All Things My Coach Taught Me & Jumping Turnstiles,** first appeared in *A taste of Hybrid Vigor: new poems of War, Passion and Social significance*. Reprinted by permission of the author. **Then One Night at Dinner** by Kate Gallagher. First appeared in *Let the Poets Speak, 2000*, Arts & Culture Committee, Town of Greenburgh. Reprinted by permission of the author. **Undisturbed** by Adrienne Hernandez. First appeared in *Let the Poets Speak*, 2002, Arts & Culture Committee, Town of Greenburgh. Reprinted by permission of the author. **Little Girls Never** by Laura Pacher North. First appeared in *Let the Poets Speak, 2004*, Arts & Culture Committee, Town of Greenburgh. Reprinted by permission of the author. By Clare Rosenfield: **The Guest,** first appeared in *Heart & Wings*. **The Guest** and **Coming Home** also appeared in *Tall Grasses of Woods Hole & Other Summery Poems*. Reprinted by permission of the author. By Margo Stever: **Tree House,** first appeared in *West Branch*. **Drought**, first published in *Folio*. **Splitting Wood**, first published in *Connecticut Review*. Reprinted by permission of the author.

Queries can be directed to Usha Akella, The Poetry Caravan, 39 South Road, White Plains, NY 10603; Email: poetrycaravan@yahoo.com; Phone: 914.686.4487

**Yuganta Press**
**6 Rushmore Circle**
**Stamford, CT 06905-1029**

# In Gratitude by Usha Akella

My first acknowledgment must be offered to the contributors—both the Poetry Caravan poets and the workshops' participants. Reading and editing this manuscript has been similar to sitting down to a sumptuous feast of many dishes. My poetry taste buds have been delightfully intrigued, stirred and tantalized! From the sublime to the spicy, the pleasure has indeed been mine to savor.

This collection materialized due to the spontaneous and generous donations from my friends, family, the Poetry Caravan poets and poetry supporters. Donations reached me from as far as the nook of South India. Without this material support, the project would have still been an unrealized goal in a corner of my soul.

There can be no mention of the Poetry Caravan without Sarah Bracey White and The Town of Greenburgh. Simply, once again, 'Thank you,' for letting me create and manifest what was once a mere intent.

The Planning Committee of the Poetry Caravan—Sarah Bracey White, Linda Simone, E.J. Antonio, Kate Gallagher and Sana Mulji Dutt—and the Poetry Caravan poets have supported me through this past year with time, suggestions, information and feedback that is integral to the success of any endeavor. Conrad Geller, Laura Pacher North and E.J. Antonio stepped in to share management tasks that enabled me to concentrate on the anthology.

Brenda Connor-Bey deserves special mention for her editorial assistance during the beginning stages of the anthology project, and for co-editing the Workshops section. Sana Mulji Dutt assisted me with more than her thorough editing and copy-editing skills. She shared my mission, and I am truly grateful for the friendship that has emerged through our collaboration. I have come to rely upon her positive support. Linda Simone stepped out of the box to perfect the manuscript with her astute proofreading skills and eye for design.

Billy Collins' participation is a boost to our project, and to have a collection introduced by him is a dream come true. From the very beginning he has extended an unreserved graciousness to our project.

To Li-Young Lee, who has the ability to transform words into a sanctuary, I offer my humble thanks.

To Kathleen Ossip and Margo Stever, our very own remarkable Westchester poets, I extend my sincere gratitude for their endorsements.

It gives me great joy that this publishing venture was undertaken by Yuganta Press. Ralph Nazareth offered untiring support and bore with my pleas for perfection. It is an honor to work with Ralph, who is not only a dedicated publisher but also a wonderful poet and trusted friend.

To name my husband Ravi would be like stating a house rests on a foundation. Considering his passion for house design, construction and interiors, I offer him this metaphorical gratitude tongue-in-cheek.

To Anannya my daughter I offer my poems.

I have leaned heavily on the moral support of my sister Veena and friend Ralph Nazareth. They were the bolsters when I needed bolstering.

It is my belief that we are able to do what we do because of the support of many known to us, and many unknown; because of many remembered and many forgotten. I offer my deepest gratitude to all those who have been part of my personal journey that culminated in this undertaking.

And neither foremost nor finally, but in constant remembrance of the Divine who allowed this work to unfold through me.

My gratitude for the journey that is the Poetry Caravan.

To the Poetry Caravan poets

# Contents

# Participating Organizations, New York 141

*Grace Church Samaritan House*
*Ruth Taylor Care Center*
*NY Presbyterian Hospital, Bloomingdale Rd*
*Sprain Brook Manor Nursing Home*
*The Esplanade*
*YWCA Affordable Housing*

# Contributors 143

# Founder's Note by Usha Akella

The word 'caravan,' brings to mind all that is itinerant, adventurous and rootless. It connotes that which belongs to all and none simultaneously. Perhaps, one could even imagine bands of gypsies—that marginalized group of wanderers at odds with the mainstream. The metaphor serves well for the image of the artist or poet in communion with other like-minded souls not traveling the beaten path.

The creative urge is irrational, resolute and simply bull-headed, making connections where least expected. It spurred the metaphysical poets to yoke the least alike objects into conceits. It prodded me to realize a vision of poets involved in society, and poetry as a medium for community service. Rather like the way one would toss a cocktail together. This past year the elements have been combined, the glass shaken and the contents stirred. The tantalizing swirl created was the Poetry Caravan—a mobile band of poets reaching out to connect, educate and entertain through what they know best—Poetry. I launched the project in October 2003 with the solid support of Sarah Bracey White, Executive Director, Arts and Culture Committee, Town of Greenburgh as an initiative of Greenburgh town, Westchester County, NY. The mission of the Poetry Caravan is *to bring poets and poetry to people in our community who cannot reach poetry on their own.* Just over one year old, the Poetry Caravan has delivered more than 70 readings and 10 writing workshops to nursing homes, healthcare facilities, senior citizens' assisted living, affordable housing and women's shelters. All programs are free to participants. Thirty-two poets have contributed their time and talent with a phenomenal spirit of volunteerism.

Consider this anthology the perky slice of citrus on the rim of the glass. *en(compass)* is the showcase of the enormous talent of the Poetry Caravan poets, and the writing workshops' attendees at the various participating institutions.

With thirty-one poets you have thirty-one halts to experience; a vast map of voice, language and interiorscape. Reading this anthology is a journey in itself wherein you can alight, muse upon and be pampered by the hospitality inherent in every poem. Open to you is an invitation to partake of the poet's quest, vision and rendering of the world. The hospitality of the Poetry Caravan poet is especially generous for this is the poetry of poets who have donated time and talent wherever there was a chance for outreach. This is the poetry of itinerant hosts traveling to share of their soul and emotions. The *Workshops* section of the book is a testimonial of their efforts.

This anthology is not flat terrain. The literary landscape of *en(compass)* is full of surprises for the poetry in this collection is not afraid to be alive. This poetry stings and sings. You may wince as you walk on shards of metaphors or feel a rush when at the edge of a thought. The nuances may fall upon you like snowflakes. You may stumble into poems like archaeological sites excavated. You will find nature and the outdoors celebrated with alert reverence. You will enter the wondrous vista of a mother's heart or walk the ragged and cobbled pavement of a daughter's love for her mother. You will find yourself in playscapes of mischievous juggling of language. Some poems are like fiery sunsets, and some will end up perching on your shoulder with nonchalance. You may experience arctic chills or ride high on sublimity and sweetness. You will find yourself in dark alleys and wounded crevices. These are poems of ascent and descent. Some will anchor you with comfort and some will set you spinning in the unfamiliar. You will find much to wonder at, much to excite you, numb you, stab you and spark your curiosity.

*en(compass)* will offer you all that a journey does, and maybe one thing more—a glimpse of your own soul. And then indeed the poets would have reached that which can be reached—you!

Travel on!

# Foreword by Billy Collins

It is one thing to write poetry and hope, as poets are likely to do, for an audience; but it is quite another to seize the initiative and take poetry to an audience, to locate and address an audience of people for whom poetry is not ordinarily available. The poets who support and foster the work of the Poetry Caravan are doing literary missionary work by bringing poetry into the lives of the often alienated residents of assisted living centers, women's shelters, senior centers and similar institutions. The choice of "caravan" for a title suggests poetry that moves from place to place instead of passively sitting still, waiting to be recognized. Here, poetry comes to its listeners and is delivered personally— a kind of "Words on Wheels."

I leaped at the invitation to add some words of introduction to this collection of poems by the Caravan poets and their workshop members not only because it struck me as an unambiguously good cause, but because my own father, who lived to 94, spent the last four years of his life at Sprain Brook Manor, a nursing home which is one of the stops on the route of the Poetry Caravan. He resided there before the caravan started rolling, so he never had the advantage of listening to this chorus of itinerate voices, but I was always grateful to the many volunteers who would visit the residence to sing, tell stories, show dogs and do any number of things to entertain the residents who were so clearly in need of stimulation and whose gratitude was palpable.

Gathered in this book, as a record of their work and a tribute to it, is a lively collection of poems by the Caravan Poets and some of their workshop students. These poems expose us to a variety of voices and forms ranging from traditional patterns such as the sonnet and the pantoum to freer modes of verse. The poems also remind us that in the realm of imaginative poetry, anything is possible. You will find here a poem that has three layers, a poet who turns into a slowly spinning mobile, a poet who walks on glaciers, and a poet who has a close encounter with a moth. The job description for a poet is not a demanding one. In fact, some wag once remarked that the hardest thing about being a poet is figuring out what to do with the other 23 and a half hours in the day. But one requirement is vigilance, for poets are observant writers who feel compelled to keep a running record of their experience, a kind of ship's log of their voyage through life. In this collection, poets pay keen attention to—among many other things—a tree house, an orange picker in Gaza, a calendar, and a painting of Picasso's. And there are a lot of poems about dogs.

Glancing through this little anthology will also remind you that poetry offers the possibility of being playful and serious at the same time. A poem may have a grave subject, but the poet is always at play with the language. And by this joining of moods, the reader is doubly engaged.

What added to my pleasure in reading these poems, as it may add to yours, was the knowledge that these expressions were not only for me the reader but for the deserving, living audiences to which they were transported by a living literary caravan.

# Poetry

# Child Poem

In a neat poem of
three-layered elegance
like a hazelnut wafer

a metaphor turns up
like a man in a kilt on
a beach playing pipes

A child appears like that
in your three-layered life of
poetry, marriage, spirituality or

India, America, identity or
marriage, love, work or
loneliness, poetry, fatigue

Just like that one day
wearing a kilt
or some incongruous costume

all her own, armful of pipes
and lung power to wake the gods
and your own sleeping heart.

# Girl

I overwrote astrology.
Where is he now?
Perhaps walking backward
from the earth—my son,
I never think of him.
Why did I want a Girl?
Why does the sky want a sun?
To will a dawn I suppose,
to break out of itself and shine
and show her own shimmering wound.

For nine months I whispered
Girl,
Every breath a flower,
every space a remembrance,
at the end of nine months
I walked in a garden
of my own desire,
How could the Gods have not smelt this perfume—
Girl.

The moment came;
my body many torn petals
my mind undone;
many fluttering wings of a moth
consumed by the flame of my body,
life lay warm at the edge of metal,
at the edge of knives the color of moonlight,
the blood.

A canvas of steel gray and helpless blood;
duotone monolith of birth in a hospital room,
and I so alive,
so alive that I knew
prophets crowded in that room,
and blessings dropped like satin or flowers or light,
my spirit soared to one point
of gratitude
for God... for Life... for being woman... for God... Thank you...
not one ravaged curse.

How could this bloody boon given be anything but woman?

4

# Fahnestock State Park Beach

Where languages fall
as ice clinks, blossoms, hibiscus;
a cocktail of slippery sounds
in the cup of my ear,
bodies slim as candles or
cigarettes pressed into sand,
out there the lake spreads, a dark ink stain
across the page of the sky
marinating in itself. She runs
towards it, her bucket as bright
as a parrot's wing,
her brown legs as new taffy
nimble in delight.
The years will await her like the lake,
she will stretch to it reach in bring in
what she can with her measure
making her own sand castles
like the rest of us.

# Man Midst Flowers

As wondrous as a 3-yr-old,
wander midst rusty-red petunias,
petulant pink impatiens,
blue tononia trumpets.

Bow before blazing-orange marigolds
shining their love straight into my soul.
Whispering sweet summer prayers,
they remember caring hands.

Whisked home, they bid welcome
to all angelic seekers and to me;
transform my manse to shining.

They'll always wake bright memories
behind my sight, with light made pure
by marigolds, as healing as any heaven.

# A Veggie's Valentine

Though artichokes may have their hearts
and green beans string along,
you're such a cute tomato type—
peas let me hear your song.

You've been the apple of my eye,
you know how much I care—
so lettuce get together
for we'd make a perfect pear.

Now, something's sure to turnip
that will show you can't be beet,
and if you carrot all for me,
let's let our tulips meet.

Don't squash my hopes and dreams,
my sweet, just be my honey dear,
or tears will fill my 'tater eyes
while bantam corn gives ear.

I'll cauliflower shop for you
for wreaths of parsley fine
and share with you my celery—
now, be my valentine.

# Building a Mobile

First of all, birth dreamshapes;
azure star-twists, golden crescents
risen up like dolphins from realms
below your sight. Silvery scimitars,
pale spirals too, cut, id-guided,
from spangled poster board
and wasted Dayglo banners.

Sprawl these out in riotous array
to tease your ordered ego and
whisk it faraway. Hang them
in sibling twos and threes
on balance-beams to twirl
like soothing constellations
above our quirky hurts.

I'd like to be a mobile,
swirling softly over
whipped audiences of earners
gentling them to rest, with
time to muse on destiny,
their wives, or other
minor matters.

## Dark and Light

we live in the present tenses
our brains divided laundry
baskets / in the dark
our every slight
devious thought
longing to belong
strapped in steel bands
never to be seen

in the light / our every joy
laugh / benevolent gifts
charity held by loosely tied
threads / the friction
of shifting strands
cuts feather fine layers
off the masquerades / to float
down the collective stream
to form contradiction's wind

that puffs the sails
of yours is not mine
arguments
blend into darks
strapped in steel
*and we have learned*
to pretend tranquility
not to spark battles

just accept
there is no resolution
to one's extreme
convictions
ingrained
in *I'm right*
and *you're not*

# Missing

somewhere inside all of us
a place is        missing

never visible to us
obvious to armchair viewers

who never move from seat
as we sort mismatched trinkets

stored somewhere inside us all
there is a sky / its ragged holes

invisible gaps full of suppose
so fine it sifts through a hair

somewhere inside all of us / missing
grew before our first gasp

our first crawl / first ice-cream / taste
our first word confused by missing

so deep it sheaths the view of color
in mist / divides self from perfection

somewhere inside us all
lives missing / as we run through time

pretending to fill the space that keeps us
breathing another day to replenish

the sieve inside all of us
wistfully hoping for satisfaction

to be on the other side
the smoother face of mountain

cliffs we slide down like children
to find the next grail / always hidden

in the sandbox / missing
continuous contentment / happy

lost in the grand illusion of quest
roaming most of the time

in the normal of restless / missing
somewhere inside all of us

# Pedestal

1/
alive in him
the fictitious
image / the good
saintly Christian
woman a lesson
in the nevers
of ritual

2/
he will not release
the unbridled
whorishness
a man and woman
need to oil
the frozen
marriage bed
unable to writhe
in relationship's
rhythms

3/
he put her
in the glossary
of his lost causes
increased ten-fold
since that wedding day
now twenty years
beyond his
reckless youth

4/
he cordoned
her off
on a pedestal
so pristine
in his mind
it equaled
the heaven
he longed
for her

5/
his heaven so high
finding her way
down to the heart
she once coveted
was impossible
as his neglect
turned her limbs
to pumice blown away
by lonely's wind / crying
for the carnal
pleasures
a woman needs
to keep living

# The Moth

The moth flew in as I closed the door,
Drawn by golden lamps I'd lit before.
I watched it flutter high, far out of reach,
Where wall and ceiling met, it found a niche.
"It's not for you, this human place."
I said aloud and gave it chase.
My apron whisked it from the wall.
Brown cloak flaring, it took the fall
and rose; eluding me then flew,
for a moment from my view.
On a fold of curtain came to rest;
Rode the billowing white and lacey crest.
"Why did you, God, permit it in?
What's better here than where it's been?
Please, help me get this moth outside alive,
Within these walls it cannot thrive."
It clung now to the inside of the door
that had provided entry just before.
I open it with aproned hand and guide,
the tentative moths steps to the other side.
And suddenly it took its airy flight
into the dark and free, familiar night.
"Go safely now," I sigh in my relief,
Glad its certain fright had been so brief.

Such fuss about a moth you're chiding me?
Truly, caring is a matter of degree.
Like Jabez* I do not want to be the cause
of pain. To anything, not even moths.
What past me crawls or flies by night and day,
I'd simply rather—gently brush away.

*1 Chronicles, Chapter 4; 9-10, NKJV Version

# Bird Ghosts

Outside, the birds flit back and forth
from pine to feeder, feeder to pine;
the every day and the winter ones
that I invite with daily seed.
The eastern sun glories in
upon my morning desk and shows,
ill-beaked and feathered detail
dusty bird ghosts on the panes.
Neither wind nor rain takes them away.

The mirror behind me on the wall
reflects it all; pines, feeder, clouds and sky.
It must seem like a place to fly to—or through
from a bird's point of view.
So they try.
But the window does not allow it.
From time to time I hear the thump that leaves
a bird ghost on the glass.

We too have unseen barriers better not to pass.
Nevertheless, we try, and do.
So much of what we see is not what it seems.
And like the birds we're often only stunned on impact,
recover, and go on.
Yet there are times a fragile life is broken;
And the thumps leave ghosts behind.

# Morning Story

The barefoot boy sat on the ground,
the sun played on his head.
A sky-blue bowl between his knees
was filled with milk and bread.

With chubby hand he fed himself
the first meal of his day.
The spoon—like little children do—
held in that awkward way.

Then from behind a sun-warmed rock,
its legless body smooth as silk,
Writhed an earth-toned garden snake,
drawn by the scent of milk.

The little child, quite unperturbed,
observed it inching near,
Then accepted its warm slither
into his lap without a fear.

From a door his mother looked,
her hand pressed to her lips,
as her boy, spoon held aloft
watched the snake take sips.

The garden creature posed no threat
to her child, the mother knew.
And then she heard that baby voice
croon, "Not *just* milk—bread *too!*"

## Geechee Daughter
*For Fahja & Zachary*

It was a shadow passing
Brief yet slow enough for her to feel
Like breaths of seaweed
Whispering in her ear

But she turned away

She's always heard them
greetings from the sea
Laughter and wisdomwords from the lady
And the man, whose footprints touched the earth
Long and narrow like hers
The crooked smile she wears as her own

But she shuts herself off now
Turns her head
Closes her eyes and ears

Old rituals in a new day
She summons without drums
Without candles
Without chants
Closed eyes, deep breaths, a shudder
And they were there

That was up north
Where shoes removed at the front door
filth of street and thoughts left outside
a life where sweeping was done in daytime only

Now hands touch the soft rise of her belly
Feels her son dancing to music he knows
Gullah songs deep within
Ocean air, mud, shrimp, crab
Whisper his biblical name
And the shadow shifts abruptly
Pulling her into the sun

*Eat crackers, chile*
*Yo mouf won't fill up*
*Wit so much water*

A high c-note splashes
Through receding tides
Beyond breakers and boats
Sees a woman holding his hand
Laughing

She smiles with open eyes
Understands

# Panama Fishing Man

I remember you made me hear laughter
instead of loud crying songs
Showed me Caribbean beats as you
placed my small feet on top of yours
dancing the meringue in a kitchen
warm with baking gingerbread

You told me
loose women feel apart
because they lost their senses

You said
"Let me teach you how
to smell the rain, girl
know when it's coming
gonna show you what a man really like
I'll show you the ocean
make you hear the songs
in the waves

You got to know dis chile
'cause every man want a woman
who know how to fish good!"

## Alice's Shoes
*For Alice Hilda McCann Connor*

Long ago when she danced 'til the sun
pushed its way through quiet darkness
Her dress flecked with gold dust
the fragrance of Evening of Paris
floated through the folds
caressing her swaying hips
You could hear her singing
when she walked through our door
tapping her shoeless silk
stockinged foot

*"I'll be down to get you
in a taxi, honey
Better be ready by half-past eight..."**

*from Dark Town Strutters Ball

19

# Beets

From my knife springs the radio,
running underneath the faucet.
Hot skin slipping off like a disguise,

stems ribbed with grit light up
in veins while a rat-tailed root-string
burrows to the center of the earth

and out the other side of the
world where another woman straps
a bomb to her belly, explodes

a restaurant by the sea. I slice
circles, add salt and butter,
cover up the dish.

Fingers dyed to match my dinner,
I turn off the faucet.
Listen to the wastewater
boil down the drain.

# Opera House In Time Of War

Fat satin patriot,
stitched in the company costume shop,
hung straight down from the roof top,
the American flag, loosely tethered,
drapes the face of the opera house, now we are at war.
Sucking, sighing, billowing,
its great belly
pooches on the night air
like a banker on a balcony
smoking his cigar.
Tuxedoed, cushioned,
in choice orchestra seats,
men weep at the final thrilling scene
as if Valhalla in flames
could lick us clean.

# I Met Two Horses

The North Sea has no direction
here. It beats the rocks on all

sides of this island. This far north,
the sky is always gray. I've come

to the end of the road. Beside me,
in a field, I see two horses

shamble knee-deep in yellow grass.
They look at me as if I were the

wild one. One nuzzles the other's
belly, then they move forward

together. Eyes on me, they stop
where the grass stops. This

is all they can do. This is
as far as they can come.

# A New York Girl Thinks of Going to Alaska

Winter for us was a couple of weekends
sliding down Gunther Avenue. We'd walk,
bundled, over Baychester's five-foot pile
where the plows had cleared a lane for cars
and clomp the six or seven blocks
in snow to our knees, to that hill,
where only two or three cars would pass
in an afternoon, heading down toward the chicken farms
where Sabina went each Sunday after church
for a raw fresh egg to give her a child (it didn't work:
she sent instead for niece after niece from Italy
to fill the gap) and where the chow-chow drooled
from huge blue gums in his folds and folds of skin,
as if some smaller beast ate him alive from inside.

Oblivious, we'd sled shrieking down the hill,
then head home, arms and legs caked with ice,
our scarves stiff around our breath.
That was winter in the Bronx.

And now I think of heading out
onto glaciers: snow and ice millennia old
in silent melt and slide.
I picture it serene and still,
without the cars and planes and people
and sirens and buildings of New York.
But all that ice is too much menace to be calm;
life there must always be on edge,
ready to slide back into chill oblivion,
ready in one shaft of sunlight to spread
roots and petals, grow quickly to seed
before the cold dark can fall.
I've bought boots—I already feel their thick
treads anchoring me to the glacier.

# Nothing is Lost

That's what the fossils teach,
leaves pressed to carbon traces,
footprints cast in pudding stone,
a dinosaur with feet smaller than my hand.
Nothing is lost, not even
what we cannot find a trace of.
Firm under our feet, those old lives
live on, in new forms, rock and root,
awareness of what we are and have come from.

Once a mind opens, the light is there;
it cannot close. Knowledge grows
and we see what we could not,
learn what needed light to be clear,
like seeds long still in sand till the rain
softens the dark, and green horns
seep through the grains toward the sun.
Nothing is lost. Everything
feeds on, is formed from the past.
And so shall we be, someday:
seed and loam for what will come.

# January—Gray Morning With Ducks

Winter ducks have settled on the river,
their white chests, white sides
outlined in black. Their black heads shine,
against the gray morning.
The usual little brown ducks
paddle around the new flock, all huddling
in the gray salt water under gray clouds.
A red tug pokes a red barge into line,
spewing dark filth into the air. The bridges
and trees are a darker gray through
the sprinkling of snowflakes in the rain.

I will the water down
through the rime
into the deepest tree roots.
They haven't had rain
like this in a decade:
a week of steady soaking,
relentless and cold,
that feeds the roots
without waking them.
It may be the saving of the trees.

It's January, the gray time after
the green and red glitter of Christmas.
The recognizable child recedes
once more to the amorphous
love that needs gray to reveal itself,
the steady pulse of tide on oil-darkened rocks,
the ducks fluffed against cold,
rocking on the ripples, the world
which exists in itself, for itself,
like Stevens' Snow Man, aside from human
needs or longing, but which awakens the vague
reaching for what hovers at the edge of our sight,
what tests the arctic boundaries
of our very human hearts.

Not all prayer is articulate;
sometimes it floats gray and still
with fluffed feathers on the chill river.

## Pigeons Hop Down Elephant Stairs

under our breaths
children beg to fill their bellies
with stories of Utopia
over and over again, to forget
tomorrow.
We have created our own Eldorado;
we have our Alice, our Snow White, our
sweet gingerbread Sundays—
and dreams of chocolate houses.
While somewhere uranium is poured
slowly into fields—over children, to
crown the Taj, and the pigeons
which hop down elephant stairs,
waiting in the Mirror House—waiting
for someone to raise a dynasty.
While we look to the sunset angels
who spread their red and yellow saris, wide
on the clouds and prepare to sleep.
We think of those who wrap
themselves in white and wait for the red angels,
wait until their skins melt into
rivers between borders;
Wagha – Amritsar;
wait for our thoughts,
of utopia,
of angels,
flying across half a century.

# I stoned the devil stoned the dream

Churned by the chants
Ka'aba stood, square,
inhaling the smell of
white cloth clinging to
a million bodies
under the sun pouring down
squirming air over
the brown hills
reaching out to touch or stop
me.
I watched them clutch small rocks
in bleeding hands and raise them
at the devil
and
I watched the blood
spurt through the first spasm
of the knife against the white
skin.
"Daddy,"
I said,
"Please don't kill the lamb.
I promise never to
dream."

# Patterns on the Floor

You were looking for colors
in our family.
      We sleep on red and yellow tiles
      to match the sunrise.
Your mother, with her

      white sari and black dyed hair
must wait—
or learn that the crimson
parting in her hair
      is offensive to
your father with his
gray beard and
unimportant shoes
      stepping on our morning
      stones.

# I Saw Myself a Tree

I saw myself a tree,
Bending in the wind,
Twisted root,
Poor soulless tree.

And I saw myself a tray
Of prosthetic eyes,
Followed a march of tears
Down the mountainside.

With shells in hand
I summoned the sound of the ocean,
Only when a palm leaf

Fell to the ground
Did I sway with the forecast,
Fall on my sword and cry
Ashamed of my deviations.

## Jumping Turnstiles

Fate makes playthings of men.
I saw the quick jump up. The young
Black belly lift and move in slow motion,
As if the boy practiced for gym class.

Jumping a horse with ease and grace without
As much as a jingle in his pocket. He cleared the obstacle
Full-bodied and swift. Even the boot chain links did not flinch.

But when the lad landed on the wine stained floor,
The M.T.A. workers had steam blasted the night before;
Time materialized another horse in the form of drug-sniffing dogs.
And the boy ran and ran, and ran and ran. Oh! See the poor boy run.

See him run. The handcuffs kept galloping, spiked teeth and all.
You must not lose track of him. He lay caged in an ambulance shaped
      coffin.
And there he lay without utterance. Nor did he reminisce about tickets.
But he stayed without moving, foot-jerking and epileptic. He was afraid to
      move or to breathe.

His skin gleamed white. Like angels' dreams of immigrants who came to
      this country dressed in poverty in search of upward mobility.
The salt tears fell like the Dead Sea rose, and cornered his eyes blind.
"Human Being" I wanted to cry out. But remained silent. As silent as the
      quarter in my pocket I pray he didn't need for his one entitled call.
Nor the words, "Watch Out, Dogs!" I may not be his color, but I'm his
      mother.
Let's call upon community to judge this deviation and punishment
      together.

# All Things My Coach Taught Me
*Dedicated to Steve Carberry*

He taught me all the rules,
To serve between the lines.
He taught me that a woman can win,
It matters where I stand.

He taught me that a net is there,
So I must pass around,
Then almost kneel, but not to pray,
To catch a yellow glare.

He taught me about love, lets, sets,
And he taught me about balls.
He says I don't need two all the time.
I have to laugh when I hear a voice say:
"Kathy, drop the balls!"

And I cross court with a childish smirk
That drips a bird from a cat within.
Sometimes I took up tennis
For my love of love, or my need of men.

Sometimes my face is like a weathervane
And I face my opponent with litmus paper skin,
Turning blue to pink then pink to blue again.
That's when I remember my coach and his prescription.

And all that is in opposition to his prescription.
That's when I remember "The Psychology of Winning!"
I leave the cackle from the dots of eyes,
And snip the ink that dares to box this pretty pink.

# Cherry Tree in Spring

Suddenly there's a chapel outside the laundry room,
dome swollen with cherry blossoms
pink, deckle edged, bunched together
swirled up towards the sun,
arched down to the earth, nodding up and down
in gentle adoration. Dark boughs
as strong as arms' embrace, split with grace
to open seats for anyone to take.
An empty blue swing with gold cords
hangs alone from a single branch
processing to the sky in lustrous pink.
This is a temple timed for breathless worship
and comfort that is swift. Inside and out
a dryer spins with clocked exactitude.
Petals feathered with a pinking shears
cling together and drop before their color
dulls. Pink radiance covers the ground
is mirrored in the silver bumper
of a parked red car. In this sanctuary
walk, dance, stand or scuff in the light
—there is no place or time for shoes.

# River Sightings

Somewhere in May a wall of old trees filled out
beyond my window, tall and overbearing
like a fence around a building site, closing off
the river with too much life. My eyes squint
through sun in search of waves connecting
mountain run-off to the bay, sweeping hidden life
to open sea; I'd rather have a gray day
when I can see platinum patches of water
through jagged frames of dull leaves.

In winter only cedars hedge my view
of currents, boats, and ice
and in the early light I catch the tides
that flow in blue, like veins beneath thin skin,
and know again
the river is still there.

# Birches in Snow

Have you noticed
when the snow falls,
stands of trees
shrink wrapped in snow
all look like birches, but you
can tell the ones
that really are.
Their top limbs have a way
of shaping branches like long fingered hands
that might reach for a pitcher
or finger the ripeness of a peach,
hands that could grab the wheel of a car
or steady a football. I've seen those branches stretch
like a hand reaching to lace fingers
through another's for just a moment
in the falling snow.

## The Seamount

Below diaphanous veils of aquamarine
the seamount rises.
Down the submerged mountain
past turbulence
to destiny's valley
body clinging
compressed by descent,
I follow one ray of moonlight
reading tide's ebb and flow
shifting currents
running the underground river of my life.

The rising water spirit descends upon me
licks salt tears locked behind my eyes;
water mirrors upside down images.
Like a ketch circling
a surface of uncertainty
memory seeks anchorage.

# Beneath Clouds

Clouds would be photographs
        out of focus;
lotus leaves waiver,
melodious balloons sound—
        frogs mating;
what love songs lie
beneath pink water lilies?
From bent trees
a silent wind drops
fragrant pinwheels.

My Western time
so out of tune with Bali
swims with heady rice wine.

In the cocktail lounge
reef kisses thunder
ocean for my companion.

# Untitled

Deep forested reef
region of the night
fish contemplate, sleep;
protected predators
envision untamed nature
from snug-fitting homes.

Unobtrusive
nocturnal wanderers
cling to scarlet sea fans
born of dark indolence
cup corals open
dip richness from the sea.

Moonlit nights
fish fear to spawn;
fluttering nudibranchs,
ladies of the night
dance: drifting into
caverns of my mind

# Nest

I take my hand
I take my hand
    hear my breath
    against my wrist
        the dry leaves grass
        the veins and twigs
        still hide me.
I have no desire to be born.

What is the
    waiting I cling to
    the hiding
        engendering hiding, enfolding
        secrets I savor
        I hold in my arms
    that pierce through the skin
lovingly.

I hold my own hand
    now for comfort
        now to stay its
        lashing out, in fists
in bones and teeth.


You ask
your questions
    with such knowing
    your mouth so sure around each
        clean oval word
        your fine wisdom
    answers
that scatter before they reach me.

You come
and shake the branch
    the wind shudders
        through the fragile mesh

                    my sheltering.
            Such is my safety
                    precarious
                            delicate as
                            the bones of my wrist
                    you grasp
    you pull as if to save me.

You pull
too hard
        and the bones
                crumble, the wind
                        pushes the branches
                moaning
        nothing but dust in your saving fingers
and the wind
quiet in your mouth.

# Under the Stairs the Silence

Dark. Quiet. The smell of
mothballs, nickels left
in woolen pockets.
Spice, the cloves I helped
to stick in dark red apples.
Smell of rain
the rubber boots, umbrellas
my father's coat sleeves brush
against my eyelids.

Push further
into the corner.
I don't need
to close my eyes here.
Darkness feathers in layers and shades
gray-black and then blacker black,
the white crack of light
against which I whisper
*Come find me now.*

Lovely and terrible, this quiet
my knees brushing my chin my hands
touch the hard-shell leather shoe tops
underneath me.
I crouch into the dark
under the stairs, my shoes the wood
creaking right above my head.
*They don't know where I am.*
I shut my eyes and someone is laughing
little girls are wicked
run up and tag you
and pout when you will not play.
Whose game this time?
*Ready or not, here I come.*

But you don't come.
I'm lost here. Or one
of the little girls is lost
one of the little girls is teasing
laughing and running away

the clapping of patent leather maryjanes
on the driveway, running
hands, dress, that keep getting dirty
the red mark
left on her cheek like a stain.
You say, What a pretty dress,
and one little girl
blushes, smiling
and one little girl cries.

Which is the one
you look for under the stairs
behind the door
inside the closet
under the dark you ruffle
the musty coats aside
and find she's not there
anymore, she's not where you left her.

# Then One Night at Dinner

I saw you
saw you first and got up oh God
out of here quickly from the table I've gotta
head down all thumbs, where's my -
and dropped it.

You saw me
saw me then and came on over
loose smiling smooth relaxed
heavier around the middle I noticed
hugging you quickly, brushing
like crumbs my heart aside
the napkin my pride at my feet.
I smile so hard my teeth
could break, my hair could
fly out raging into flame.

*I rush at you*
*heat and wind*
*my body into you shatters*

Hey, you say so natural as if this were
you're so magnanimous pleasant
your easy going swag, your brush-casual
J. Crew wrinkled academic look
your eyes I once crawled into, there
as if over coffee light as a breeze.

Can't move.
Me, I
can't breathe can't pin you
loud with a stare to nail you to
the spot you sail so sweetly from.
Hollow in my blank
my stare my legs attached to this smile
now frozen in place.

But laugh on easy and say Let's
as if we ever could or wanted to.
Now your long loping

slide on back to your table where you
smile, again, so easily
at her.

*Want to hate*
*you break you*

Then
somehow I
must have picked up my wallet
the crumbs my heart
the wrinkled napkin, tired suddenly
now quiet now the burning
leaves me empty.

# Another Example

In Sumatra Marco Polo saw a creature with a single black horn
in the middle of its head and thought it was a unicorn.
Didn't he know a unicorn's horn was supposed to be white?
Plus the beast wasn't gentle enough to be spending time nuzzling
a maiden's lap or gazing into mirrors alas, alack.
Marco said it was a unicorn even after it went on the attack
crushing some animals and ripping them with its sharp and spiny tongue,
which would be sure to send any sensible maiden on the run.

Maybe M.P. got his tapestries wrong. Maybe he was deranged from fever.
Who can blame him for trying to comfort himself with familiar shapes?
In strange surroundings, we might do the same to say nothing
of all the circumstances in which ah, desire!
We misconstrue the scene before our eyes and stumble into fable.
It's the elephant story told wide-eye.
Marco saw that horn and couldn't help but lie.

# Open Air
*For Bill who suggested writing poetry outdoors*

I sit very still in the garden and wait for words.
What comes this afternoon is a yellow and blue Fritillary
landing at eye level on the Buddleia bush, so close
I see its hair thin tube unfurl
and for long seconds imagine invisible sipping.
Then a mourning Cloak flies in, dun brown until
bright spots flash from pulsing wings.
Riding a tenuous branch that sways under whisper weight,
it nudges the other and both butterflies spiral away,
circling like the lexicon in my head,
eluding vision or coherence.

***

At five p.m. a rabbit, ears up,
stands in outline against the grass
as in medieval tapestry—rangy back legs, white tail,
fur reddish on the neck, black bead of an eye.
Is this mild creature the executioner that has lopped
the orange and yellow headdress off my fiesta daisies?
Stripped of ornament, seedless among the plantings,
those spare stalks tell suspicion plain.
I wait, but grazing daintily, the rabbit's softly twitching
muzzle doesn't approach the flowers,
and I am reminded of surprise, memory edging
wordlessly from the mind to blossom into speech.

***

Being still, still being, I am learning

—that the grove of lavender
scents the garden
but the small rosemary bush
pushes its pungency through

—that no matter how still I sit, the catbird
jabbers in indignation at my presence
and when I talk back
flies up into the dogwood and meows.

—that if I hadn't been watching
I would have missed
the sudden darting of a hummingbird,
never seen before at the butterfly bush.

# Wondering Eye

These days when eyes shudder
awake to flesh scraped
from walls and trees,
and streets are blood,
I dream a sudden
radiance of birds, flowers.

Two golden winged blackbirds,
fly into my sight,
a painted oriole sings,
and a bower of yellow roses
opens to the sun.

What is it but a hope
that somewhere peace prevails.
If for the sake of knowledge
the snake was set in the garden
why, after expulsion, few are wise?

These songs, these vibrant roses will not stay.
Clutch at them, risk the silence,
the loosening calyx,
the hardening light.

Like Eden, a temporary place,
gift of a dream, no more no less,
this wondering eye,
this birdsong heart.

## Undisturbed

Fashioned against the blue sky
Barren branches bend and sway
Brown, broken leaves below
Circle like scurrying squirrels
Yet
Amidst the flurry
A blackbird
With lacquered feathers
Sits
Undisturbed

# On the Cusp of Sleep and Wakefulness

Beads of freezing rain
strike the pavement
like handfuls of rice
after a wedding.
Irregular rhythms
like an ancient song
soothe, awaken
mesmerize.

I
in flannel robe
sip tea
light candles
string together
words
like beads of ice
forming a rosary.

## To an Old Love

It was fall
But the apple tree bore no fruit
Content to separate
Sunlight into shadows

We were young
Yin and yang in faded jeans
How we clung to each other
Like monkeys to a cloth mother

I see you as you were
Hazel eyes squinting
Brown beard, the color of bark
Garnished with gray

I've kept as a relic
Your wire rimmed glasses
Wished I'd apologized
For breaking them in anger

Three decades gone now
Crows shiver in the tree
And debate such issues
As their immortality

I sit alone
With a pocket full of change
Unmatched socks
And a teacup filled with rain

# A Mausoleum with Closets

My husband bought a double cemetery plot
    before he died.
He wanted to make sure I would be
    beside him for eternity.
But I have other choices.
    I am a veteran and can be buried in
        Arlington Cemetery.
    My mother and father have a place for
        me in New Jersey.
    There is a lovely cemetery across
        the road from where I live.
        The trees are lovely in the spring.

But what I really want is a Mausoleum.
    A mausoleum with windows
    and lots and lots of closets.
I want to take everything with me.
    I want to take my books, my music,
        my paintings.
    I want to take my clothes, my hats,
        my shoes.
    I want to take all the baby pictures
        my Mother's Day cards
        the recipes I've saved and
            haven't used
    and that pile of newspapers
        I haven't read
    I want to take my favorite chair and my
        living room rug
    I think it will look nice up there
I want to take everything
I'm an accumulator and have lots of stuff.

But is it not absurd to think others will treasure
    all you leave behind
My daughter lives faraway, very busy
She will have no time to sort
    what to keep and what to discard

She will simply call the Salvation Army
and they will cart everything away.

# He Never Took Her to Dinner

He never took her
    To dinner
    She had nothing
        to wear.

Just long black wavy hair.

She defied the almighty
    and listened
    to the snake.
And Adam of the apple
    did willingly partake.

They were banished
    from Eden
to fend for themselves.
and found the elements
    hard to take.

So they went
    shopping at Loehmann's
To find something
    to wear
Now Adam takes her to Dinner
Everywhere.

# Rye Beach

I often drive to Rye Beach
    which is not too faraway
    to walk and sit on the boardwalk.

On that cold—crisp—clear day
    huddled in my coat my hat pulled down
    and my collar up to my ears.

I sat fascinated watching
    a patch of shimmering water
    shining in the Sun.

A cluster of sparkling stars
    had dropped out of the sky
    still floating on rippling waves.

The tide was out and on the water's edge
    a string of large footsteps
    left deep in the sand.

Not a soul in sight
    when the tide comes in
    all the tracks will be washed away.

Now I sit watching a flock of white seagulls
    with their puffed up breasts,
    and their skinny little legs at the water's edge
        resting in the sand.
    Each in place in their own space,
    all turned toward the sun.

Suddenly I notice
    on my right
    a courting dance

A male bird circling a female round and round
    she ignores his intent and gives no heed
        to his passion spent
    just lifts up and flies away.

Was his libido so aroused
    he dare defy nature's plan?
    This was NOT the time of season to mate
        or to propagate.

In Ecclesiastes it states
    *"To everything there is a season*
    *And a time for every purpose."*
    This was NOT the time to copulate!

## Cycle of Life

We met, we looked, we loved,
　　　　we wed,
It was our time we said.

Then came the children with all
　　　　their care,
It was their time we said.

Parents grew old, and we were there,
　　　　It was their time we said.

Then the bonuses did appear,
　　　　our grandchildren were here,
It was their time we said.

And now they are grown and on
　　　　their way,
And now it is our time we say.

# Conversation

Conversation is becoming a bore,
I don't want to hear it anymore.
Don't tell me your Aunt Suzy
has the gout,
That's not what I want
to hear about!
And don't tell me about
your trip to Timbuktu,
Unless I've been there too.
Don't tell me
your cholesterol is 199,
When you know I'm
struggling to lower mine!
Don't talk and talk,
And talk and talk
while I sit there
like a dork!
Tell me about
a book you've read,
Or a play you've seen
that I might think
is kind of keen.
Ask me if I'd like to eat
and then we'll pick
a place to meet.
Conversation can be fun
when the topic is a mutual one.

# To the Ladies

When we were in our thirties
we were at our peak,
In our 40s and 50s
some cosmetic help we did seek.

Then we hit our 60s and
liposuction trimmed bellies thin,
But when we reached our 70s
we knew old age had set in.

Thanks to modern surgery
we were able to go on,
A knee, a hip or cataracts
were fixed with great aplomb.

For those reaching 80
who plan to stay around,
Your future's guaranteed
to be safe and sound.

All your parts have been repaired
so you can say with a smile,
Hello world, here I am,
I am good for another 2000 miles.

## Picasso's Portrait of Madame Z

Within my mouth the Eastern dainties melt;
The Moorish world arises with the taste,
In all its long-gone splendor and its waste
Of Spain, when there my father's father dwelt.
Long buried deep, asleep, obscure it lay
In all my veins' hot-coursing Spanish blood.
Madame, though you are French, I sense a flood
Of yearning to paint you in a Moor's array.
Borrowed: the trousers, fez, and veil. The face
Alone, Jacqueline, that is your very own—
Your eyes, your mouth—the cares of nowadays—
A roof, some food—traced faithfully thereon;
To keep fixed here and now my brush, my gaze,
Lest too far back into the past I roam.

# The Wake

Too late we brake! The damage had been done,
The small wake was attending to the corpse:
The anguished mate, or paramour or
Whatever nomenclature fits in squirreldom,
Dumb—not understanding immobility—
Not so the crow! He let it be known
He was the legatee, the rich inheritance
Was his to feast on, flesh and entrails, his!
With every passing car,
The two recede
Only to reassemble about the corpse,
Which lay bloodied on its side with one cocked paw
To salute its love, to fend against the beak and claw.

# William Foxwell Albright

Massive main. Spacious mouth to encompass
All those sounds of all those alien tongues.
With large chest, thick throat, and full-toned voice,
He recited a monologue that led us
Along the path trodden by Abram when
With his ancient Aramaean nomads
He was called forth from Haran,
By way of Egypt,
To the promised land of Canaan;
Spoke of the raised, stayed knife of Abraham
By Isaac's body bound upon the stone.

Scholarly: They say he could date
Thousand year-old fragments to within fifteen years.
So deeply steeped in holy Pentateuch
(*Smiling he told this story on himself*)
That addressing a Galilean crowd—
In Hebrew—when speaking about the Lord
He termed Him "hashem"—the Name—but careful
Not to name the Name.
And they—the crowd there—
Couldn't comprehend the euphemism
And wondered what the man was speaking of.

Now this seventy-seven year-old frame
Will lie beneath the surgeon's hand and knife
Which won't be stayed,
Which may or may not save
The vision of this legend of his time.

# The Pickle Room

"It takes time to season things,"
Grandma groused, shooing us away,

as with grave step she bent toward
the acrid dimness of the pickle room.

A servant girl, her gloomy vanguard,
fanned her path to keep the flies

from garnishing the puckered mangos
jammed in forty thieving vats.

Together they'd unseal the lids,
peel away the spice-soaked muslin

(a glowing sheet of pearly mold,)
and lift the river rocks of ages

tamping down the brew. With ladles
long enough to row a floating shrine,

she'd stir the wells of hot and sour
with breathless murmuring and chant,

treading ancient ways she may not bend,
and then with ceremonious care

lay across the mouths full buxom moons
of virgin cloth again, reset the lids bossed

and burnt with dates fired in a kiln,
there to rest for long forgotten seasons

of rains and heat and jasmine nights,
waiting as one always waits for life

and gifts of melons, babies, brides
from goddesses and summer mothers

to fall laughing in our laps before
we dip into the pickled world.

# Questions for Eleni

What's this they tell me about the light of Greece?
Why does your igneous rock turn to marble and alabaster?
What can you tell me about the birds of your land?
Do they all have the gift of prophecy?
Your lambs and goats, sheep and bulls--
do they turn into lovers in spring?
Does their blood turn into wine?
And what about your little mosses, ivy and other creepers,
do they speak of things your philosophers know nothing of?
What can you tell me about your gods?
Why would I care?
Except, how can I not feel
I am also Leda splayed on the ground,
my heart the opening for their shuddering torsos?
Would you believe if I told you
I am the secret lover of Lysistrata,
the one who whispered into her ear
the secret of stopping men's madness?
Tell me, do young men in Greece sleep with their mothers?
Is this why mothers tear their sons limb from limb
while they're still tender and lovely?
Do fathers in Greece eat their own sons in their blindness?
And what about sons and their simmering hatred?
Are there more important things for me to know
about your land of the blue glass mirror and the wine dark sea?
Please open the box and let me in on the secrets.
Or would you rather not be Pandora?

I am more simple than you think I am.
I am more frightened than I let on.
I am more unknowing than mitochondria.

Like you, I also want to speak
to simple people in the marketplace.
I also dream of hills that return my song to me.
The sisters who stand entwined against the wind—
I know them well.
I am a baby crawling in a roomful of things
looking for a key, a hammer, a pen.

They are nowhere to be found amid the rubble of the world,
so I put my fist in my mouth and eat my heart out.

I know my India no better than I know your Greece.
Ignorance is my name and my belly's full of desire.

## The Eyes of Gaza

In Beit Hanun in steaming Gaza,
the orange trees are bulldozed,
acres of aged creatures on their sides.
A woman gathers the oranges,
eyes of the fallen, dead yet sweet with juice.

Who am I but a distant spectator
standing on a hill at a safe distance?
Yet it must be told: yesterday it was the olive
groves, today it is the fields of oranges.
Tomorrow, as always, scraggly little Davids
will throw pebbles at Goliath tanks.
The sky is opened and mountains laid low.
Is it birth they await or is it death?

Fields stretch with the story of the world,
kids frolic among bales of hay.
A cloud kisses the ground in pitiful homage,
a mud house in ruins shapes the horizon.

In the middle of this who can remember
the universe is ours to make and re-make?

In the dark fields light flashes
incandescent on copper plates.
School buses glow red in the distance
as babies are bodily assumed
into heaven, their laughter immortal.

I wander through arcades and penny fountains.
In lit green bowls
delicacies for the tongue and eye
decked with sprigs of coriander.
We've not lived and loved until
our yearning for warm places
for the mountain's edge
for the falls of snow
for the depth of the earth is satisfied,
until we've said Yes to this creation
that hungers for our touch,
to be imagined, seen, eaten

just so, just so
without fabrication in the fifth dimension
without the false plastering of crimson
on the colorless
just so just so

with the authentic frozen gaze of the one
who singly conquered the North Pole--
not a thought for us who toil in the foothills.
He knows only of height, beauty, and heart,
knowing deep in the marrow
that free of our eye, desire, design
there's nothing worth caring for,
there is nothing.

But give me the shoes dangling on electric wires
any day in place of the arctic gaze,
shoes that get there via a fling, a flight,
a twirling in the air, the twinkling of an eye-
hand coordination, a perfect snaring,
give me children in windows, cheering, making faces,
their soft fat bodies against crossed bars
hooting at life down in streets of red bricks
baked by years of sun and sin.

Let the arctic stew in its own deep freeze
and let us drive without design
past the raped olive groves and orange fields
past the midnight machetes
past the terror of the axe
arching down in slow motion,

keep moving on in the streets of our desire
lips speckled with crumbs
cheeks shining with juice

toward nothing
but hope.

## Kodiak Love

The bear that is my heart
    stumbles restlessly
    when you are not around.
Without a hint of your scent
    it is sentenced
    to no rest.
Clumsy as a cub
    roaming blindly about,
    it's happy once again
    in the comfort
    of your den.

# Younger Brother

Have I ever told you
    that I loved you
    from the moment
    I saw the crown
    of your little baby head?
We don't share memories
    in our family anymore.
(*But, then, did we ever?*)

This is how it was.
You were born on a Monday,
    brought home on a Saturday.
    —liquid bullets of rain
    sprayed the sidewalk
    all day.
The welcoming party
    of few
Sat in a borrowed car
    listening to the drear,
    the father
    isolated in an envelope
    of illness and fear,
    the others
    waiting for something
    to mend them again.
The back door opened
    and you were handed in,
    protected solicitously
    from your too-new world.
Arms argued over
    who would get you first.
When it was my turn
    I buried my nose in your milky smell
    and kissed your downy head.
It was the first time
    I'd ever known
    "love at first sight."

The car ferried them home
        in the onslaught of rain,
        the father cast adrift
        and heading to the whirlpool
that would soon
        pull him down.
And though his legacy
to this baby
        would be scant
        —little joy
        —unspoken words
        —unshared events
He folded this baby
        into his heart to take with him
        on the journey he still faced
        —this son
        whose birth he'd overshadowed
        —this child whose portrait
        was his mirror.

Have I ever told you
        that I loved you
        from the moment
        I saw the crown
of your little baby head?

## Little Girls Never

Watch how you sit…keep your knees closed…
As if a view of between your legs
would let the world in on
all your better-kept secrets
And so it goes
As the child becomes the woman…
Look good—but not necessarily as who you are.
Learn to use false eyelashes
and false flattery
because that is what empowers you.
Never mind your lineage
—generations who
    have birthed both warriors and artists
    since time began.
Worry rather that
    you will become like Samson shorn
    when you wrinkle and gray,
    powerless to attract,
    a fertile vessel no more.
But you know that you are more than that
    —more than a flawless face
    —more than an opening and closing vagina.
You knew it when you were still that little girl.

# I Have No Way of Equating Letters into a Math Solution

Living for the moment is tough enough
to dream is okay
but to go back several seconds ago
is not possible
and yet math professors
science buffs
and imaginary minds
delve into its possibility

could it be a perfect person
wanting to readjust a fault
displayed in a frozen frame of the past
erase mistakes already performed?

the mystery of space
fuels the imagination
we can see distant stars
but cannot touch them
we vision the black night
but are unable to reach its tips

the mind reads the past
mentally sinks into the adventures
with the safety nets of the present
makes believe
with equal gusto of the moment

then opens the eyes
to face life

and the unknown

# Inherited

We are the product of our producers
from inner feelings to inner structures and outer features
the crinkled black and white photos
display their physicality
but not their deep emotions
that was given to me
my feelings are the evidence
in what I show in my actions and spoken words
done without thought seen without comparing

we are we

and yet we erupt our thoughts with the minds of the past
that are buried inside us
I look at the aged photos of my parents
but I know not of their emotions
I have no memory
just the physical hand-me-downs

their history vanished
when influenza took my mother
and the strains of the years of the depression
overwhelmed my father
as for my love
their care given to me
I gave to my children
and in return
they to theirs
with my deepest devotion

some of what my mother had I too have
it is the one thing from my father
that stands out and cannot be denied
I inherited
my father's ears.

## Sometimes

Sometimes
I find it difficult to act nice
with animals it's easy
most times they are looking for food
nose to the ground searching
eyes to the sky always alert
trying to avoid being the searched

most times I mind my own business
when it comes to the animal kingdom
show care for the small ones
deliberately avoid the larger beasts
that always seem hungry
or are content just licking their paws
I become a coward when I see ferocity

never knowing their reaction
when seeing me
I not wanting to tempt them
or become the ultimate food filler
become weary and leery
I am afraid to appease the fates

so I avoid the wild ones large and small
only make nice to puppies
kittens and an occasional bunny
I pet them with much care

but also go ugh to spiders
little crawly things
and snake-like creatures
adding lizards and dragons
to the—to be avoided—list
never knowing
their true reactions towards me
and my precious body

I do that to some humans too
as we get closer
to election day

# First Christmas After

Pivoting in the cascading snows of winter,
I left the nucleus of a family
As we traveled separate paths.

Now we touch like paper wrapping
and as far away as home, I mold cookie
dough with my grown daughter,
making tapestries of green trees.

I trace garlands, split and bruised
like dreams, remember dolls that filled
my house with Christmas clatter.

Beside her single "Nancy" stocking, my daughter
fastens my "Karen" stocking to her California
condo fireplace. With every cookie tree
I cut, I feel my fingers slide over each new edge.

# Missing Sam

I will explore missing Sam in fourteen lines.
Call it my sacred sonnet with too many rhymes
I see a cloud cone of ice cream settling in a Western sky
Echoes of light mask the view from one eye
I greet joy in a birth belting out a happy cry,
A multiplicity of sounds seeking harmony from one
Stretches on my path like a kite floating high.
I embrace life that slides by me in a quilt of smiles.
Reciting 'Humpty Dumpty' over a clatter of miles
Cradling the phone before making a candid remark
I dream Sam is waiting for me in the dark.
I watch clouds in the sky that wrinkle the sun
I listen for the miracle of Sam's sweet cry
It squeezes my own voice as a comforting sigh.

# A Pantoum About Hair

Hair scatters in the snow
My back turns
from the mess
Birds gently sweep it up.

Do not weep as
hair scatters in the snow
I see a few strands
from the mess.

Wisps caught in gloves
Do not weep
The cold razor snips and coils
I seek a few strands.

Clumps of brown
Wisps caught in gloves
Birds build warm nests
The cold razor snips and coils.

Remnants in a hat
Clumps of brown
escape from me
Birds build warm nests.

I weave another life
Remnants in a hat
Mouth open, sighs
escape from me.

A temporary solution
I weave another life
Echoes of healing
Mouth open, sighs.

Round dome wrapped tight
A temporary solution
hides downy fuzz, new growth
Echoes of healing.

## The Guest

The immaculate makes room
for the newborn.
She loves her handiwork.
Mystery sings crickets in her ears.
She inhales and a door swings open.
A large rocking chair invites her to sit.
Hinges fall away.
Silence, crickets, breath rock the baby.
The Guest will stay awhile,
perhaps the whole night long.

# Snowy World

I meander a magical street where
antler arms hold
puff-ball damsels
who glisten like tinsel,
sway in the moonlight,
glow in the whitened night
I point my face into,
crunch my boots under,
sing my heart out for
transformation is the magic
snow waves like a wand
over everything
and the world stands up as one.

For once
white is not a color
which divides.

# Coming Home

Beloved,
I worship your night sky.
I moved all of my things
out of the way
to put my face up against yours.

Your night creatures tickle my ear-space.

How can I sleep
when I have just awakened?
There is so much living to do.
I taste your kiss.

# Bojangles of the Bunkers

Towering over me as we talked
In a beat-up black overcoat
Gloves without fingers
A hat that said "Pittsburgh"
A cane covered with colored rags;

We whiled away the day on a bright sunny morn
He told stories
I told stories

He showed me pictures of his adopted kids in Vietnam
And back and forth we wove our conversation

When I mentioned music his eyes lit up
"I'm a musician," he said
I played with the bombs flying overhead

Toward the end of our talk
He confessed he was going into a home

He had no family
And the richness of his life
Had spilled out to a total stranger
I left him bereft
Knowing I would never run to him
To share more stories,

Bojangles of the bunkers.

# This is how we got the Jews out of Yemen

Living in blessed innocence of aviation
Old men prayed
And pregnant women murmured

Then they remembered The Books of Isaiah
"And they shall rise up on the wings of eagles."
They boarded the big bird to the land of milk and honey
This is the power of our bible stories
Like a monkey wrench in the imagination
They kick in for us
When we need them most.

## Sister, Sister

Beware the hour
When girls get together
To drink tea and read poetry;

Revolutions are underway
Tables are tilting and spinning and turning into eternity

Steam rises from the savanna
We're reading tea leaves and dreams

Sister, sister
Hold onto my secrets
So my soul won't fly apart

I'm speaking of secrets and spelling out dreams
We're handing out sentences
(Judgment day may be on its way)

We're fighting with crutches
I don't have to hand you a gun
For you to teach me to fight

I've been defending the territories of others
Now I'm fighting for my own
And only my own

My defense is with hammers and nails
And houses and children who grow strong

I'm not reading lips now
I'm not missing stitches

Lipstick is sticking to teacups
Cooking pots clanging in harmony
From kitchen to kitchen we're telling stories

Sister, don't sit alone on nights like this
Nights like this are to light candles, say prayers
And walk away from slavery forever.

# Waiting for the Elevator at the Esplanade Home for Seniors

At the Esplanade, we're stuck on 15,
Four people out of time—
two residents, two poets.
Elevator button set aglow,
we wait, watch floor numbers like a firefly
on slow rise to adolescence.

Herb says, *You're stuck!*
*Everyone's going to lunch.*
Bert (not Bertha) says, *Write a poem*
*about it!* We laugh, wait,
eye that firefly grow younger.
Alice mentally calculates

her parking ticket. Herb bursts
into lines from Longfellow—
We listen, forget, remember
that kind of power.

Bell sounds and in piles Herb—
his walker like a VW bug,
Bert with her beautiful mink
hair, Alice reaching for keys
and me calculating inches of piling snow.

In this chariot with no muzak,
Herb says: *Key to happiness*
*in an institution? Who you eat with!*
*I'll remember that,* I say. On M,
Herb and Bert alight, wave, fade off.
At L, Alice and I part ways, beam—
never stuck in the first place.

# Fuji Apples

He walks away
from the basket,
snaps the plastic bag like a towel
just pulled from the line.

He palms apples, speckled,
red like a sunburn.
One by one he gathers them
for me

Somehow it's the same
as taking home
Mount Fuji—
just because I want it.

## from *Voice Lessons*

We all can be found out
by the map we carry: junctures of our words,
the singular river of our song;
ranges of our thoughts.
On this journey of acquisition
we leave voice-prints—
but what we desire speaks louder than our words:
Who seeks money?
        Who wants toys?
                Who lives for love?
Who hates it here?
        Who longs for voice?

# Reporting on *Dog Poetry*

On June 18, 2004, just shy of the "dog days of summer," I pilot-tested a new program for the Poetry Caravan to connect poetry and people. Together with Sr. Ruth Dowd, the Dean of Graduate & Professional Studies at Manhattanville College, we read a wide range of poems about dogs by famous and emerging poets. The spotlight, however, was on Dudley, a trained therapy dachshund owned by Sr. Dowd.

More than 25 residents of The Esplanade turned out for the poetry and Dudley's repertoire of tricks—including "high five" and "dead dog." Some people in the audience reminisced about their own favorite family pet as they reached out to give Dudley a scratch behind the ear. The only complaint was that they wanted Dudley's company a little longer.

# Tool Parts Chest

Seeing my grandmother, Nonnie, like that.
The rush of scenes up and down the years,
makes me dizzy.

After seeing her,
bought the chest for twelve ninety eight
at Home Depot tonight
Two bread boxes big.

Black metal sides, rectangular shape
holding forty
neat clear plastic drawers,
deep with stops to let them lay angled
when opened.

Pull drawers out, put in nails,
screws, nuts, and stuff
sorted by type and size
so my wife and I
can get to them more easily
saving time when they are needed.

Two and a half hours tonight
sorting out the mess accumulated
Pouring boxes of mixed mess
onto cardboard.

Picking out small metal things,
gathering them in my palm,
then putting them into their drawers,
designated by me with
Post-it strips on which I
hand-print headings.
Finishing nails - small, finishing nails - long,
wood screws - countersunk, wood screws - round head,
machine screws - small, machine screws – large,
nuts, bolts, nuts and bolts,
washers,

on and on,
Sorting, labeling, putting.

Mom's been caring for her big-time
Dad's depressed by her dementia
which grows over the monitor
in the living room
picking up her voice on the other
side of the wall.
Finished. Organized. Done.
Too bad too late.
Few times I do handyman tasks now.

Will try to see her tomorrow morning.
She didn't remember me yesterday
twenty minutes after I left.

Should have spent more mornings
with her before she lost so much
of her mind.
Should have had more mornings of
coffee and home fries,
listening to her stories,
hearing her sing old songs
she handwrote on
the wide-ruled white pages of the
black-marbled composition book holding
her past.
Sing them to me Nonnie,
I'm ready now.
I'm listening now.

# Happy on His Shoulder

At that brown Formica dining room table
There he was
my Grandpa in his fifties

Sitting at the head
Telling us stories
We the grandchildren, children, sisters
        and brothers and their offspring

Grandpa was happy to hold court
in his house with
his family
and his family was happy to listen
and share the togetherness

No matter the content
each story was an eye-opener
and told a tale with a twist
and often a moral,
a lesson on living life

Perched on his left shoulder
the parakeet named Happy
listened to Grandpa's every word

Every few minutes
Grandpa sliced a piece from
a red apple
and without looking
handed it to Happy
who cheerfully pecked at it
glad to be with us
the human family

who all were enraptured,
loving Grandpa,
listening,
eager for the next morsel.

## Lost Illusions

The sign was cardboard, 11" by seven
with green crayoned words
"Lost illusions"
all upper case
with an exclamation mark
ending the upward drift of letters

Bright green string
held the placard around his neck
dirty and undefined from
the grime of his tattered shirt
hanging on shoulders at least seventy-five
years of age

One pot collecting money
was filled with fives and tens
no coins with them

The other pot held folded notes
I supposed describing the donors' written
lost illusions

When he turned his head
I put a twenty into one pot
and took 3 scraps from the other

For an instant I felt like a thief
But I reasoned I might read
the note and try to make
each of three lost illusions
a found reality

The three are still in my jacket pocket
Tomorrow I plan to open them.

## My Mother Learns English

Anxious immigrant at 64, my mother is learning English.
Pulling rubbery cinnamon-tinged hose to a roll beneath her knees,
and sporting one Baptist ski slope of a hat,
she rides the rattling elevated to a steel spire in downtown Chi,
pulls back her gulp as the glass elevator hurtles upward
and comes to sit at a gleaming oak table
across from a pinstriped benevolent white angel
who has dedicated two hours a week
to straightening black afflicted tongues.
It is this woman's job to scrape the moist infection
of Aliceville, Alabama from my mother's throat.
*I want to talk right before I die* my mother says,
*Want to stop saying 'ain't' and ' done been' like i don't have no sense.*
*I done lived too long to be stupid, acting like I just got off the boat.*

My mother has never been on a boat.

But 50 years ago, a million of her, clutching strapped suitcases,
Jet magazines and peppery chicken wings in waxed paper,
stepped off hot rumbling buses at northern depots
and eagerly brushed the stubborn red dust from their shoes.
"We North now," they all said, slow backdoor syllable,
as if those three words were vessels big enough to hold
dreams that spilled over the borders of sleeping,
my mother's Chicago dreams, simple but huge.

She thought it a modern miracle to live in a box
stacked upon other boxes, where
every surface reeked of Lysol and effort, and chubby
roaches, cross-eyed with spray, dragged themselves across
freshly washed dishes, dropped dizzily from the ceiling
into our food, our beds. Mama's huge dream required
starch stiff pinafores, orlon sweaters with stitched roses
and A-line skirts in the color of winter. There had to be
a corner tavern with a jukebox where bluesmen begged
forgiveness in gravel bass, and where mama could perch
on a comfortable stool by the door and look like a Christian
who was just leaving. There had to be a job that didn't involve

soil or laundry, where she could work in a
straight line with other women, *repedida, repedida, repedida,*
no talking allowed, their heads drooping with big dreams.
There had to be a Baptist church where she could pull on
the pure white gloves of service and wail to the rafters
when she felt the hot hand of the Holy Ghost insistent at the
small of her back. He had blessed her journey so far,
quickened her step, stroked her free of the Delta. She was His child,
building herself anew in this land of scorch and bleach. And she'd
given up wearing pants because the church said she should.

Her calling was to curse a comb through my wiry hair,
nag me to sit up straight, pinch my nose sharp,
lead me to Jesus and grab the switch when I sassed.
She didn't talk unless talking was called for. I assaulted my father
with my dreams. Now she says it hurt when I gave him everything.

When he was murdered, almost 25 years ago, mama and I gazed at
each other across a yawning chasm, harboring no idea
one about the other. Except this.

I know she doesn't believe men ever landed on the moon,
that the whole thing was staged in Arizona someplace
because *American folks are stupid that way and always will be.*
I know she only thinks she is dying soon, because it is
fashionable when you are old and black and Baptist
to think so. I know that I never realized
that the way she spoke
was ever a problem
for anyone
especially her
especially me

My mother's voice:
It's like cornbread, buttery and full of places for heat to hide.
When she is angry, it curls into a fist and punches straight out.
When she is scared, it gathers strength and turns practical, matter-of-
     fact, like when she calls
her daughter to say *they found your father this morning, someone shot him
     and he is very dead.*

She can't sing, not at all. Her voice cracks and collapses and loses all
     acquaintance with a key,

92

and every Sunday morning it's my mother's
voice you hear, unleashed, unapologetic and creaking toward glory.

When my mama talks, the sound of it is flat and broad and wild with
     unexpected flowers,
like fields in Alabama.

She has never been grammatically correct. Her rap is peppered with *aint
     gots* and *I done beens*
and *he be's* the way mine is when I'm sweet color among colores and
     don't have to worry
about being graded. I see no shame in this.

Her dreams for the most part realized, my mother now
stashes away dollars to pay for her own coffin, not wanting to
bother me, as she says, *with that nonsense.* She instructs me not to
spend too much on the service but sternly relates the story of
the lazy daughter who neglected details,
so her dead mother's body was sent to church #1 while
everyone waited to mourn in church #2, and *If that happened,
chile, I'd be so embarrassed.* No mother, I think, you would
be so *dead*, but I don't dare bring this thought to voice
because Annie Pearl Smith is not a fan of humor.
When she retired after 40 years making malted milk balls,
hot dog gum and candy corn, it was a whole year before
she could scrub the stark smell of sugar out of her skin.

Turns out now that my mother's most persistent dream
is to wash history from her throat, to talk like a woman
got some sense and future, to talk English instead
of talking
wrong.

I pick up the phone these days
and there she is,
precisely using her new mouth.
She slips sometimes, but she
is proud of what she remembers, and it pains to hear her effort,
the sum of all her dreams whizzing us back to that moment
50 years ago, on the Greyhound bus rolling north from Alabama—
my southern mother in one seat, dead since Memphis,
and my northern mother in the seat next to gone self,
wondering if any coffin will be big enough.

93

# When Dexter King Met James Earl Ray

There was a tender in them both, a place picked raw.
As Southern men do, the clasping of hands that know
weather. Eye linked to eye, unflinching, the flat-toned,
muttered how-do. How do you? And the scripted respect,
the pudge-cheeked preacher inquiring idly after the dying
man's days. Whole wars in them, but just a single rupture.
Their halos florid, overglowing, some news reporter hissing
expectantly into a dead silver mic: Say it, *say it*. James Earl
liver-toned, wobbling on old bone, one lazy eye perked for
it. *It.* The King is rolling his Rs, throating elegant, sweating
bullets into his collar. Having shaved too closely, his beard
is peppered red, whispering blood. And still the pleasantries.
Exactly how does one go from commenting on the weather
(it's hot: awfully humid: smells like rain: hope it lets up) to
asking did you frame my father's head in your gun sight, did
you empty his dinner chair, lonely my nights, pull back on
that trigger? *Jesus, he looks just like his nigga daddy,* James Earl
thinks, hopefully not aloud this time. *Bet he can call on God
and turn his other cheek with the best of them. Go on, get it out.
I'm dying heah.* Cameras whir. The men are like fools, silent,
damned respectful, exactly a yardstick between them.
And it's the windup, the pitch: Sir I have to ask you, my sir,
my kind sir, excuse me, I hate to bother you sir, but I have to
ask for the record, *Did you kill my father?* And if the answer
is yes, will there be a throttling, an errant sob, a small silver
pistol slipped from an inside pocket? And if the answer
is no, will there be a throttling, an errant sob, a small silver
pistol slipped from an inside pocket? Time has a way of
growing things all huge. But, surprisingly, James Earl resists
spittle and the wide-eye. *No, I didn't. No. No.* That settles it
then, that settles it. And we're locked in on this limp drama
long after the credits have rolled and Hollywood Squares has
taken over, long after the network has signed off and clicked
into morning snow. Time for a Twinkie and a beer. Time to fall
asleep with a clear head. Time to celebrate the slow sweet of
Southern men. It's time to rejoice in the fact that nobody killed
nobody, and high time to forget that somebody died anyway.

# Tree House

Something about roots,
boney, tenacious,
that grip the moving ground,
the branches like umbrellas
bent back and broken by the storm,
the leaves' veined references
to hands, and the sound of the wind's
wild workings against them.
The boy collected the branches
and stored them under his bed.

Something about the tree seeped
into his dreams, the trunk a hallway,
the branches outlined rooms,
and his family finding shelter
in the boughs, listening
to the sound language of leaves.
He did not see a garden, apples, or any fires.
Everyone huddled together to keep warm.

# Drought

A dry spell
shimmers on the page;
heat burns off words.
Useless articles
pile up like trash.
I plow them into hills.
Small silences, words like
"it" and "but" clatter together
in memory of what's
unexpressed. Reassembled,
they could be bones, meadows,
offerings to the gods.

Here is a mound of bones,
woman with infant,
a modern living sculpture.
Her breasts are wilted.
Below bellowing surfaces
that cry out for food,
angular bones
pierce through papery flesh.

The verbs linger longest,
out of alignment, months later,
hardest to forget. They knock together,
lonely for ancient villages,
the specificity of snow.
A thousand times each day
I think of death,
the villages of people
on their knees, sowing
children into rows like seeds.

The mother and child starve.
Leaves on the trees blur
behind their backs.
I stare out of windows
for signs of passing shadows,
but the neighborhood looks the same;
houses set on foundations,

people pose mutely behind closed doors.
The rancid glow of streetlights
colors the road with hollowness,
the line in the middle
almost lost in the glare.

# Splitting Wood

It was the thought of his entering
their infant's room that drove her.

She remembered his face the first time
she saw him. Now half gone from whiskey,
eyes hooded like a hawk's,
he said he'd kill the children when he woke.
The neighbors heard it before,
the screams. They heard.

His workingman's hand,
his gnarled hand dangled down.
The knife lay by the bed.
She slipped from the covers
while he slept, placed her feet
on the floorboards just so.

The dogs barked outside, snapdragons,
flowered tongues, and all the wired
faces of the past strung up. The ax
hung on the porch, wood pile nearby,
each log plotted, uneasily entwined.
The children's tears were rain,
tears were watering the parched hills.
The wild moon foamed at the mouth.
The wild moon crept softly at her feet.

The arms that grabbed the ax
were not her own,
that hugged it to her heart
while he slept were not hers,
the cold blade sinking in his skin.
She grew up in the country splitting wood.
She knew just how much it took
to bring a limb down.

I have always had an interest in poetry from childhood. As a student in the first grade, we had to learn nursery rhymes and I felt that they were little poems, and expressed joy to the listener. I cannot write poems but I love reading them and I have been asked by many persons to do a reading on programs. Poems tell stories of adventure, lifestyles, love, sorrow, patriotism, wars, religion, and all aspects of life. I try to express what the poet writes, and I admire their works.

# Charlie at Four

Whatever happened to my puppy?
> The mischievous and funny Charlie
> He grew up in a day
> Or instantaneously as some say
> > Not kidding
> From one day to another
> My pup became a Dog
> I said Oh my God!
> I trained this pup well
> And he is swell!
> At four years of age
> Independent and brave
> Charlie learned his bag of tricks
> Nothing makes him tick
> Nonchalantly lounging
> On all my furnishing
> Waking up for walks and people talks
> And of course food
> And depending on his mood
> Will follow me or not
> But mostly keeps to his spot
> Not heeling with me from room to room
> And letting me his hair groom
> I don't recognize my puppy!
> I trained him to be
> The mature dog he is now
> What a change, Wow!
> Couldn't do without him
> More than ever
> Since he is so clever
> And he learned so well
> Good manners…
> Yet not letting a passerby come too close at night
> And protecting me tight
> For intelligent he is
> In Dog types, a Wiz
> From mixed breed of course
> With a paw a little coarse

Since I stepped on it last night
What would I do if I had a Chihuahua
Instead of this solid uah uah…

# Dreaming

A ride in the hay
Bless this day
No compromise
No surprise

A fever blocks me inside
Except for canine duties
I meditate on holiday coming soon
With or without a full moon

Would love a carriage and horse
On terrain that is coarse
With a dog at my feet
Totally asleep

And look at the skies, and the firmament
                              of stars
With a sigh of relief and lament
The deepness of a being is hard to understand
I often withstand
And get back to a dog or a hog
While the Infinity lies in our souls and this starry night…

# Jealousy

Life had become unlivable in the large white space
And the opal bird became supreme in the cage
With quite a bit of rage

Even if picked at the same time, same place as Turquesa
He didn't let the poor baby eat, drink or fly
I understood the coming plight
And had to return him to the store
With my throat all sore
Swallowing the sand of departures

Later on Charlie came into my life (Turquea is seven)
Expressing his confusion and agony
When I touched the cage it was almost felony
He was jealous…
And tried overturning the stand by walking underneath it
Being smart and a pup, Charlie
Learned not to depreciate the birdie
Still nowadays
When I sing or play with parakeet
Charlie gives me a pleading look and tries to get me off the hook
Of bird and cage
So he grabs a toy and runs, I behind, our favorite game
And Turquesa, amused, chirps away

This Dog won't attack a feebler one
As nations of men do.

## One Dead Afternoon

my daughter asks me between bites of her sandwich
where I would like to be cremated, here or in India
"You don't mind my asking about death, do you?"
I had settled for the mother-daughter-daily-chat scenario
forever, but my dead body rears up between us,
cutting my youth short.

"Here, of course." "Not India?" she asks, surprised.
"It's too complicated for you to cart my body across."
I don't tell her that dragging me through customs,
baggage claim, and taxi stands to the pyre
might leave her very few sweet memories of us;
nightmares of bodies sitting up in flames is hell.

"But it's so mechanical here—a few minutes
in a machine and you're ash." A leafless branch
scratches itself lazily on the window behind her.
"Exactly," I reply. "No mess. I like that."

# Colors of Rain

Rain on gloomy days is gray,
sometimes silver against red maple.

It is steel, stainless, luminous
when the street lights flare at dawn
and the dark hasn't quite crept away.

I imagine rain holding back surprises
on days when not a drop has touched the earth.
My Pakistani neighbor shakes his head,
looking up at the cloudless blue,
"My vegetables need rain. Muggy nights,
a few showers, only then the soil will catch."

I don't tell him I wait for rain, too,
to perceive its hues. Somehow,
the aesthetic holds no logic—
it hangs unsaid in the air between us.

But I suppose farmers in my grandfather's fields
contemplated the colors of rain as they prayed,
sent up offerings in smoke so the thick, sweet
moisture may fall in time, break the sigh.

I imagine them standing among rows of paddy,
eyes, mouths, ears open to silver thundering down.
One more harvest!

Last time in a train rushing through wet green,
it was still day and the drops were eggplant;
as the day wore on, the rain was coffee, dark.
I stretched my hand to feel the needles tattoo me.

## Unholy Laws

My mother-in-law is visiting from Delhi,
a big place, to our little apartment in New York.
She shifts pots and pans to establish her way
among paper goods, trash can, microwave.
When she awakens, the clocks set their time,
rituals blaze in every cranny. From our balcony
above the pines flutters her holy sari in icy wind.
She is satisfied when a lock clicks into place.

My mother-in-law stops the new moon in its
orbit, starts it back on so it matches my period.
I am her guest three days of the month
when she places morsels three feet from my futon.
She believes that women should hide anger.
Cooking is our sole duty, it replaces sex eventually.

Evenings we hold up the express line in King Kullen,
bags of cilantro and chayote on the counter,
the cashier's polished nails drumming steel,
while my mother-in-law chats with other mothers-
in-law from Madras, Bombay, Karachi.
She tells them she is doing her motherly duty
by visiting her son. To get back, God willing,
to one's own soil, to die in one's own cot!

# Fledgling

The morning hit my window, lit the room
with aviary peeps and sounds of clacks
of trains in distant stations moving crowds
to other places, leaving some behind
to wave and melt into the shadow.

The bird within me knew a fledgling was
about to fly, to gather all her years,
then set them down in unfamiliar spaces,
perhaps to bounce upon a breeze and feel
the freedom of her wings, to glide upon

her own maturity, to dance with strangers.
We hardly talked, just passed each other by
and went about the preparation for
her flight. The morning passed us by and it
was noon. The birds outside had quit their peeps.

The heavy traffic in the streets had hushed
the sounds of distant trains when it was time
for her to fly. We packed the car with all
her years, some Teddy bears and toys, some grown-
up clothes and shoes, clean underwear and shirts.

And off she went. I watched her go. She dis-
appeared around the curving road. I waved
and waved until my arm was sore, then held
my breath, exhaled as it began to rain,
then melted in the shadow of my nest.

# Past the Year 2000

Pages of the calendar have
turned a thousand times
between January and December.

Radios and cell phones
decorate the ears of passers by.
Snow and rain have cleansed
the streets of the last century.

The ball has dropped, cheered
by crowds that come and go,
faceless on Broadway,

not here when you and I
danced hand in hand
on those same streets.

We danced out of town
and up the Hudson Valley
against the estuary's tide

where you were swept away.

# The Porch
*(The Depression years through the lens of Walker Evans)*

The day, folded into shadow.
The self, swallowed in dryness,
decaying wooden planks and walls,
unpaned windows, unhinged doors.
The earth, burned, turned to sand.
Your blue jeans worn as working clothes,
no fashion, your children's bare feet
walk the barren fields in hunger.

Your stare distant, empty stomached
waiting for a war to come three years
down the road, to grow the cotton,
sow the corn. Three years down the road
boys will leave the porch in uniform.
You hold your hands in resignation.
Shadows fill the house, darkness of the
hunger years in your daughter's eyes.

Your life, flattened in two
dimension, black and white,
hung on museum walls.
The scene bares no relation to
images upon the silver screen,
no dancing feet, no frilly furs
no happy ending.

# Writing Workshops

# Esplanade Assisted Living Center

Now that the Poetry Caravan has been through two phases, I continue to be touched and inspired by the many participants in the workshops I facilitate. Sharing poems with the participants at the Esplanade Assisted Living Center has been a remarkable experience. Each session was filled with this sharing through poems, of memories, dreams, tears, laughter and hugs. Each participant gave something so powerful that carrying those poems and words in my heart became a significant source of inspiration for me.

As you read through the poems that the participants chose to share, you will see why this venture is so special to me. It reinforces my belief every day in the power of poetry to enhance, heal and transform lives.

# Please don't treat me like I'm old

Please don't treat me like I'm old
Or I'll pretend you're right as rain
My brain is good, my knee is bent
My walker takes me like a train

I need my glasses to read and see
I use my hearing aids when I arise
My dental bridge must be installed
And eye drops go into my eyes

I count out six whole pills to swallow
I break my teeth and mouthwash drink
A bit of spray on graying hair
And at the mirror I bravely wink!

## Blocks

What are you able to build
           with your blocks?
Houses and gables and shoes
           and socks
Down stuffed pillows and
           footstools galore
Places to meet read write
           and more!

## Through the years – yard sale

I'd like to sell the trials and
           tribulations of yesterday
And fill the future gaps with joys
           and laughter the rest of the way

## Please don't treat me like I'm old

What does that mean?
Old is precious
Just like gold
As years unfold
Old is bold
Precisely wise
Without disguise
Do treat me like I'm old
           and
Respect all that you are told.

# If I had my life to live over again

If I had my life to live over again
There are things I'd repeat
And things I'd delete
I'd pick the same man to be my mate
Why change the thing that was so great!


# A tree house

A tree house, a me house
A house I'd call my own
Away from the sound of the city
Away from the ringing of the phone
I'd just relax in silence
I wouldn't think of all the violence
In the world that should be free.


# I am an old woman

I am an old woman and I feel that as
I am able to I will teach
Right now it's
Affected my speech.

# I like to think that I'm not old

I like to think that I'm not old.
Could do the things from former years
I liked to dance and swim
I liked to bake and decorated all
      my cakes
Today I look back and all these
      happenings
Am glad that I did them and
      enjoyed them
So please do not think that I
      am too old to still
Enjoy many things that
I still could do today.

# To my great-grandson, Steven

Steven is playing with pillows
He pulls them here, he pulls them there
All of a sudden there is his castle
And he and his sister are creeping in it
All of a sudden they laugh and stand
And the castle comes down with a bang!

# Cane-proof!

I have a cane
But I do not like to use it
it stands in the corner
and I like to think I am
cane-proof!

# If the world was crazy

If the world was crazy
You know what I'd do?
I'd publish a letter
And say that I knew
It ought to be better
For in my view
It's crazy already
I'd like it more steady
Wouldn't you?

I think it would be slick
If no one were sick
If no one grew old
Or ever felt cold
It streets ran with gold
If none knew hunger
And we would keep growing younger.

# When I am an old woman

When I am an old woman
I shall wear more color than ever before
And try to continue to have
Some coordination to my
Appearance

Growing old is mostly a state of mind
Why should I change my habits now?

Since I have more ailments than
Ever before I shall try to practice
Better eating habits and take better
Care of my body

Why must I change? Now this
Is the last time around so I

Have to make the best of everything!
Even if it takes more effort.


# Yard sale

Now is the time to take stock!
How important were the things
I pondered over to buy
And spent sleepless nights over this and that
Only *things* I say to myself now
Did it give me pleasure, yes then.
But now watching my husband choosing a suit
And tie would be my pleasure
My grandchildren's visits and phone calls
Are most of my pleasures today
All the material things and I had many
Are superfluous now. I begin to
Realize the real meaning of life and
The important things, love sharing and friendship.

## Potatoes

Potatoes remind me of many things
How I loved to bake them
How I hated to mash them
But all in all I miss the smell from the oven when they
Were done and all the family
meals they were served at

Scalloped potatoes, potatoes anna
Potato latkes all bring back a memory or two.


## When I am an old woman

When I am an old woman
I shall enjoy the laughter
And silliness of my wonderful grandchildren
And have the pleasure of seeing
Them grow up to mature
Good men and women.

## No inspiration

A potato in my hand
Course and smooth to hold
It feels so rare
So light and fair
Can it feel so grand
and round and bare,
While it is still rare?

## The Potato

It is a wonderful vegetable
That can be transformed
Into many delicious
Dishes, such as potato
Latkes, kugels, soups, we like it,
But it doesn't like us!

## Yard sale

A garage sale including my piano
I haven't had time for my piano
When I was 8 years old I was the only
Pianist in my school
There was the conductor in the auditorium
And she chose me to accompany her
There I was at a seven foot stairway
Walter Damrock heard me play
For three years and he said to me
"See me when you graduate from college."
So I decided not to sell my own piano
and instead gave it to my daughter Joyce.

# Poetry Afternoons at the Alcohol Rehabilitation Center

I was a bit worried to find out that each of the counselors at the Alcohol Rehabilitation Center had been ordered to round up a client or two for my Tuesday afternoon poetry workshop. We ended up with nine men, one woman, and a counselor, assigned, I suppose, to rescue me in case of utter disaster. My opening shot, "Does anyone have a poem we can look at?" was met with uneasy stares, but I was ready for that. A long, eventful teaching career had conditioned me never to rely on chance, and I had prepared some poems I thought the group might like to look at.

I have always been convinced that good poetry is better than bad poetry because it can engage the ordinary listener immediately. In my definition that is, in fact, what makes it good poetry. I know from experience that poetry should be able to speak for itself. Besides, most people know when they're being patronized and they resent it.

I began with "Richard Corey." No one had the slightest difficulty understanding it, and the group seemed interested when I pointed out the poet's careful choice of words ("imperiously," "people on the pavement").

Suddenly one of the men said, "Here's something I made up a while ago." It was a long, confessional poem in couplets, rap style, about what he had learned from his mistakes in life. His ear for meter was perfect, and he didn't falter in the long recitation of it.

The others were unrestrained in their praise. I had taken some notes on the diction and, when I ventured a critical comment he asked, "Have you ever been in rehab?"

"No."

"Then you can't understand what I'm saying."

"Well," I said, "isn't the purpose of poetry to cut across the lines set up between people and communicate with them?" The reader saw immediately that that's what he wanted to do all along. It led to a lively discussion of the uses of poetry and the ways school so often subverts it.

After that it was easy going.

In subsequent sessions we looked at works by such diverse poets as Lucille Clifton, e.e. cummings, and we even looked over a Shakespeare sonnet. By the third session, however, there was little time for the poems I brought because the members were starting to recite their own poems, mostly composed in the familiar strong iambic tetrameter of rap poetry.

All in all, I learned something about what poetry still means in the lives of ordinary people, my own relation to it, and, best of all, that the old girl is very much alive.

## Reflections on Teaching Poetry at Grace Church Samaritan House

The reluctance with which the women approached the poetry workshop and the contrasting moments of joy and confidence with which they concluded the workshop told me the story of what happens in a poetry workshop, especially with women who are most frequently voiceless. While some participants discovered their own facility with words and images, all participants had the chance to recognize beauty and truth in their own experiences and observations. Listening to and creating poetry fosters the imagination, something I believe to be especially useful for participants dealing with the struggles that brought them to the shelter.

## Tomatoes

Salads, salsa, but I'm allergic.
I like the redness, the softness when you squeeze them.
The taste-what is it? Sweet? Tart?
It could be sour sometimes - the acid in them.
The kind that taste like cardboard they put in sandwiches
sliced very thin so you can chew them
and you won't notice that taste.
Tomatoes have a fragrance, but it's hard to describe.
My neighbor raised them on the north side of Mount Vernon,
used dog dirt to fertilize them, made them very big.

## Stairs

The stairs here aren't easy to climb.
You feel your weight coming up or coming down.
In the dark you could slip coming up here,
bump into people coming or going.
Sometimes I feel I could fall on the stairs.
It's better going out than coming in. Sometimes
you get a rush going down the stairs
and opening the door to go out.
I was in New York City today on nice clean stairs-no urine.
Some people have phobias about stairs.

## Shoes

When I was pregnant with my son
I was in a class where you had to teach someone
how to tie a shoe.
I said I'll tell my son how to tie his shoe.
"No," they said, "that's not it."
I had to teach him first – I couldn't just tell him.

# Daffodils

I don't know what a daffodil is.
It's a flower with yellow on it.
My uncle used to make wine from them.
Maybe that was dandelions—they're yellow too.
My cousin tied daffodils together to make a lei
The way they do in Hawaii.


# Cats

Meow. Purr. I don't like them.
I guess I have to get used to them.
If I raised a cat on my own I'd be very sensitive.
I wouldn't want my cat to sneeze on babies.
I like them when they're frisky.
When my mother was knitting
The Tabby we had would play with the yarn.
I can see it.

# Courage

I need a lot of courage.
I haven't had much of it lately
stewing in my own sorrow the last week or so.
I'm coming out of my shell slowly,
like a snail peeking out,
feeling the sun rays on my head.
I like that.
It can't get any worse 'cause
I have just enough strive to make it better,
enough courage to put those short term goals into play,
enough courage not to use again.
That's how I feel today.

# Seeing My Mother Today

Let's do this real quick.
The woman who birthed me.
who gave me life, I look like her.
I even talk like her, but I'm not her.
She put these buttons here
so she can push them when she wants to.
I put buttons there too so I can push them
when I want to.
Today was a nice day seeing my mother,
the woman I call mother.
I gave her a kiss, said hello.
She gave me a hug and said, "you're fat."
The woman I call my mother
I love her dearly
but it's good we don't live together.
The woman I call my mother took me to lunch
and took a long time to say she loved me.
The woman I call my mother. I'm her last born
and I gave her so much hell coming out
she hasn't let me forget it
for forty years.

## My Daughter

The way she turns from me to the father
who's not her father but gives her everything,
it eats me up like the plague,
like AIDS,
like cancer.
My insides get tight,
so tight they feel like they'll burst.
But she's not where she needs to be
for me to tell her how I feel
but I wrote all the hurts down in a journal
For her to read and know
how I feel.


## Birds Before Rain

You know how birds are just before it rains.
In the park in Peekskill I'd watch them all gather,
mostly blackbirds making noise.
I'd wait and wait to see what's going to happen.
I'd wait and watch to see why
the birds were staying there in the trees talking.
It felt like something very big was going to happen
and they knew it.
Maybe the sky was going to fall
or the rain pour down so hard you couldn't see anything.
I never waited long enough to see
why the blackbirds gathered. I never waited long enough
to see why they did what they did.

# The Mouse

Mice are cute.
Once I kept one as a pet.
He was there
and he (or she) just wanted someone
to play with.
I'd chase him over the sofa
and he'd keep jumping
over the rest of the furniture.
I could never catch him, he was so small.
But they set traps in that building
and someone caught him.
I didn't see him anymore.
A mouse very would go right through you.

# Grace Church Samaritan House Workshop

It was enlightening to teach my first class at the Grace Church Samaritan House with a group of young women who had had very hard lives—substance abuse, jail, estrangement from their children, homelessness. We were all a bit nervous. But they were remarkably attentive as we began to come up with images that expressed strong emotions, making the images visual, tangible, real. Gradually, as we began to put those images together, something magical happened. Their eyes lit up. There was a poem, and they had created it, using simple but carefully chosen words, and they saw the remarkable beauty in those words that so perfectly expressed what they felt. There was beauty even in sadness and rage, and the poem had meaning not just for the poet, but for others as well.

Through the Poetry Caravan, we, as teachers and poets, reach out and share our experience with poetry, inevitably sharing our lives. We hope to enrich even just one person's life, or maybe just their day, even just one hour. But the thing about this process is that it works both ways. Sometimes I'm not sure who benefits most—me or the participants. The excitement of reading, talking, flashing on new ideas, trying something that seems crazy—is infectious. The joy spreads. And we find that what we've shared is more than just ink on paper.

# Pearl Ring

Did you ever know someone
so fascinating it was a wonder?
Were you ever so touched
by a gift that you cried?

Eyes closed, hands held out.
Tiny box placed in palms.
Eyes open, surprise!

Black pearl ring
not one but two
not white but black
perfect fit
questions asked
answers heard
my other half dove into the sea
to recover pearls
to make into a ring
for a woman he hoped he would meet.

Tears flow
smile forming.
That's what it's like to be loved.

# Glass

A glass and stone cathedral,
cut glass windows and doors
an arco iris of colors,
dazzling brightly from the suns rays
continuously from dawn till dusk.

Visitors from around the globe
long to visit the cathedral of many colors.

Inside, priceless ancient crystal chandeliers
hanging high above the pews.
Goblets of white and gold glass
shine triumphantly
glittering in the translucent light.

This beautiful gem-encrusted sculpture
stands strong through the seasons
500 or more years.
Time has been benevolent.

Future generations will gaze upon
and admire this tower of glass and stone
the Cathedral of many colors.

# Esplanade Senior Living Center

As a Poetry Caravan poet, the connections I've made at the Esplanade Senior Living Center in White Plains have provided me with a fulfilling interactive process of sharing feelings, words, and memories. I realize that teaching the writing workshops to the senior residents gives the seniors a voice and recognition of the important role they still have in our community and society as a whole. As we share words, their wisdom leaps across the page in profound ways.

I've been presenting a variety of poems whose themes touch upon memories about gifts received, celebrating parents, honoring flowers, and appreciating music. As the seniors respond to the poems in writing and discussions with me, they gather further understanding of themselves and their remembered experiences. The social and emotional benefits derived from their self-expression are rewarding for all of us.

Recently, to commemorate Father's Day, we wrote in response to father poems that produced heartfelt memories from a long time ago. As a representative of the Poetry Caravan, I feel our mission is continuously achieved as we reach out to those Westchester residents who want to explore their creative talents through poetry and writing workshops, and who would otherwise not have the opportunity.

# Grace Church Samaritan House Workshop

*Poetry is an orphan of silence.*
*The words never quite equal the experience behind them.*
Charles Simic

I taught a poetry writing workshop at Grace Church Samaritan House on four Saturdays. I wasn't sure what to expect, but what I found were women who loved poetry, loved to read it and chew on its meaning. At our first class, I read this quote by Thomas Gray: "*Poetry is thoughts that breathe, and words that burn.*" Hearing that, the women said, "Yes, that's it. That's right!"

We worked in an area that was both kitchen and TV room and had a small bookshelf. At each session, we would read aloud several poems that I brought in—poems by Elizabeth Bishop, Gwendolyn Brooks, Billy Collins, Jane Kenyon and others—and we would discuss them. Then the women would write their own poems and share them with the group.

Their poems were so real, their voices so unique. Louella wrote about how she disliked it when she did not have a destination. Claire wrote about swimming, saying:
*Seeing under the surface*
*One only feels light*
*and no weight*

I took the poems home to type and place in a binder for their bookshelf.

On the evaluation forms, one woman wrote that poetry meant "a release of some of my feelings, which means a lot to me." Another said the workshop "was a nice and quiet, relaxing time." For me, these workshops gave me the chance to get to know a handful of women whom I would never have met, the chance to hear their hearts—which moved mine.

# Swimming

I missed it.
For quite a while.
Now I see why.
Breaking against the water,
that first dip
the speed of lap number one
seeing other gliders
in nearby lanes.
Knowing about the muscles
being used.
I am doing something
good for myself.
The different strokes.
Seeing under the surface.
One only feels light
and no weight.
Good for the heart,
good for the mind
the heated pool on a cold day.
Who wouldn't want to learn?
The feeling of accomplishment...
Swimming.

# What I like to do

I listen to all types of music.
It takes me through time, defines
part of me, a lot that I like
to remember.
I like jazz and rock,
R&B, drums. I always
want to dance an African parade
and go to an opera.
Country's no joke either.


# What I don't like to do

I was walking without a destination.
When I was a kid and would set
out with my sister, I was the kid
with no destination.
Walking for hours, only she would know
where we were going
I would ask over and over.

Stop here at the store, meat market,
say hello to this person and that,
and inside, I would feel anger
not knowing. And to this day
I would not go anywhere
without a definite destination.

I just stay still.
Smell of car exhaust, perfume, dead meat.
Car horns, noisy people,
kids crying because they are hungry.
*Let's go home now, please.*

# T-Shirt

There was a T-shirt
I got once that my
case manager sent to me
by mistake.
It was a man's. I had
to wear clothes
intended for a man...a man's things.
I cried, got angry – stuck
in here with no clothes
and to be seen in men's clothes.
I wonder what the man
said when he got my
women's clothes. What
*did* he say? Sorry.
I kept that T-shirt
for 15 years.

# The Egg Cups

The egg cups had a history of their own.
The Captain's wife still had two of the
     original eight.
Five generations ago, a noble couple
received eight egg cups as a wedding present.
A grandmother had been given
     six of eight egg cups designed with gold
     and brightly embroidered, enamel colored flowers.
Six cups had crossed the Atlantic
     with grandmother and her new husband.
The eldest daughter was given a
     gift of four of six egg cups and after much time
     passed, two egg cups to one of
     her daughters after her engagement.
Although the two egg cups remained
through wars, fires and natural
disaster, they, of course, were broken
dirtied up, were cleaned, moved to and fro
but, nonetheless, are well mended
like that of a broken heart. Time
heals most wounds.

# Participating Organizations

### Grace Church Samaritan House

*The Poetry Caravan has been a wonderful addition to our program of community services here at Samaritan House. We are pleased that the Caravan will continue to bring its many voices of hope and inspiration to our women—and that they will be able to contribute their own voices to the Caravan as they did this past year.*

*The Poetry Caravan has proven to be a wonderful venue of exploration and expression for homeless women who are unnoticed and voiceless.*

**Carrie Robinson, Director**

### Ruth Taylor Care Center

*The Poetry Caravan has been a welcome addition to the Recreation Therapy program at the Taylor Care Center. The poets have been friendly, professional, personable, and have fostered a wonderful rapport with our residents. Their monthly visits are eagerly anticipated, and a loyal following has developed among the Taylor Care residents.*

**Rich Fetzer, Director Recreation & Expressive Therapy**

### NY Presbyterian Hospital, Bloomingdale Rd

*We are so excited about the Poetry Caravan coming to New York-Presbyterian Hospital. We recognize this invaluable opportunity: talented poets who will share with our patients their poetry readings—both personal works and selected readings from famous poets. Thank you again for providing this gift!*

**Laurel Torres, Volunteer Services**

### Sprain Brook Manor Nursing Home

*One of the things that residents look forward to when the Caravan comes to the facility is the energy that a poet exhibits while reading his/her poetry. Residents feel that it brings out the true essence of the poem and allows them to paint a better picture in their mind as to the content of the poem. Overall, the residents enjoy a change of pace as well as culture coming into the building—and the poets offer that!*

**Jeff Pryluck, Director of Recreation**

### The Esplanade

*I would like to thank the Poetry Caravan for their kind and generous contribution to our senior population. Our seniors enjoy the poetry readings which are done monthly. The readings appear to reach them at a very deep level which is so important to their well being. The writing workshops have been a great success in helping the seniors learn to express themselves and release emotions.*

**Mary Carter, Director of Recreation**

### YWCA Affordable Housing

*The YWCA of White Plains and Central Westchester operates a supportive housing residence, which provides permanent housing to 177 single women. The community is diverse in its talents and life challenges that the women bring through the front door. We house only low income women who work hard to achieve their personal goals of health, mental health, better jobs, higher education, and independence.*

*The Poetry Caravan has provided a unique service to the women of the YWCA residence by assisting tenants to explore their feelings and express themselves creatively through Poetry writing workshops and readings. Classes have been conducted on a flexible schedule to meet the changing needs of our tenancy, and the women have loved it. They particularly like the professional instructors, who are seasoned poets and kind teachers. I whole-heartedly support the efforts of Poetry Caravan, and look forward to a future of collaboration.*

**Lori A. Stanlick, CSW, Associate Executive Director**

# Contributors

**Usha Akella** is the founder of the Poetry Caravan, a volunteer organization that takes poetry readings and workshops to people who cannot otherwise attend such events. She is the author of a book of poetry "*...Kali Dances. So Do I...*" She performs her Sufi poetry accompanied by Steve Gorn on the flute throughout the tri-state metropolitan area. She has read at venues such as Omega Institute, The Hudson Valley Writer's Center and Philadelphia Museum of Art.

**Jay Albrecht** describes himself as 'eternally-curious.' He has explored Swedish lakes, Moscow's subways, art galleries from the Met to the Hermitage and Moderna Museet, fixed cars and bettered egos, written villanelles and publicity, built mobiles and cutting machines, swum amongst morays and penned love poems on tablecloths. He has read his poetry in NYC, Westchester and on local radio. His work has been published in the US and Swedish Mensa Journals and other literary journals. He has published two chapbooks. It is his belief that, "...students of all ages, encouraged by an understanding teacher, can poetically express their feelings, hopes and behavior in a spirit of exploration and fun ... while improving their communication skills."

**E.J. Antonio** resides in Mount Vernon, NY and is one of the founding committee members of *The Poetry Caravan*. She has attended the Sarah Lawrence College Writer's Conference and has completed two Cave Canem New York regional workshops. E.J. has appeared as a featured reader in the New York metropolitan area. Her work has also been featured online at Poetz.com, RogueScholars.com, and LouderArts.com and has been printed in numerous anthologies. She has placed second in the Annual Greenburgh Poetry Competition in 2003 and 2004. She is currently working on a full-length manuscript and a chapbook.

**Caroline Baisch** is a poet with the Poetry Caravan. She is a mother of three and grandmother of eight. Although born in Brooklyn NY, she has lived her entire life in Westchester. She recalls being a winner in a Seventeen magazine poetry contest fifty-five years ago. She has had six essays published in the Journal News. She has retired from Readers Digest as an editorial correspondent.

**Brenda Connor-Bey** is an award winning poet, writer and arts-in-education consultant and is a co-founder of New Renaissance Writers Guild, founder of MenWem Writers Workshop and a member of the Harlem Writers' Workshop and the Poetry Caravan. In 2002, she was awarded the Outstanding Arts Educator Award from the Westchester Fund for Women and Girls. She is a recipient of a CAPS award for poetry, four PEN awards for non-fiction, a NYFA for fiction and is a MacDowell, YADDO and Cave Canem Fellow. Her first book, *Thoughts of an Everyday Woman/An Unfinished Urban Folktale,* is a collection of prose and poetry. She recently completed a chapbook of poetry, *Spirit Seeker,* and is currently working on a novel, *The House on Blackwell Lane* and a young-adult novel, *Adventures in the Land of Purple.* Recently, Brenda became a member of the Board of Directors of the Hudson Valley Writers' Center.

**Michael Carman** is a poet, novelist, and teacher. Her poetry has appeared or is forthcoming in *Rattapallax, Space & Time, Lumina, For the Gathering*, and online at nycBigCityLit.com, and she has read as a featured poet at various venues in the New York City area. Michael has taught writing in prisons and to ex-offenders in residential

143

treatment centers, and currently teaches in and serves as coordinating consultant for a series of creative writing workshop for seniors in Manhattan under the auspices of Poets & Writers. She served as senior poetry editor of *Lumina*, the graduate literary magazine of Sarah Lawrence College, where she completed her MFA in poetry last May. She is co-founder, with Vicki Moss, of the *Borderline Poetry Café*, a new readings series at the Irvington Public Library.

**M. Doretta Cornell** is a Sister of the Divine Compassion and Associate Professor of English at Pace University, Pleasantville, New York. She is a poet with The Poetry Caravan

**Sana Mulji Dutt** is currently training for her Certificate in Poetry Therapy. She has facilitated poetry workshops at the Esplanade Assisted Living Center in White Plains, the Nyack Library, the Clarkstown Senior Center, Nyack Elementary School and is currently facilitating the YWCA Affordable Housing workshops.

**Kathryn Fazio** was named Poet Laureate of the College of Staten Island, CUNY where she won the Ed Rehberg Prize for Poetry and the Ferrara Scholarship from the Performing and Creative Arts Department. Her poems have been published in numerous literary anthologies as well as other poetry magazines. Ms. Fazio has been featured on several radio shows in the New York metropolitan area. She also appeared on Brooklyn Cable show, Earth is Not On Tape, it's companion CD series, and the Manhattan Cable show Earthbird.

**Alice V. Feeley, RDC**, a native of Brooklyn, NY, has taught at the elementary, high school and college levels. Currently, Alice Feeley is President of the Sisters of the Divine Compassion, White Plains. Alice began writing poetry about twelve years ago and has had some of poems published, e.g., *America*, *Inkwell*, and *in\*tense* magazines as well as *Let the Poets Speak*. Alice won first prize in the adult division of the 2003 Greenburgh Arts Council Poetry Contest and delivered an original commemorative poem on 9/11/03 at a groundbreaking ceremony in Hartsdale for the wall of tiles created by local residents in response to the tragedy of 9/11.

**Helene Fishman** is a wife, mother, grandmother, daughter, scuba diver, photographer, gardener, observer and listener. A trained social worker, she has been writing poetry in fits and starts since the third grade. She is interested in world news so that she understands that local news or squabbles can be unimportant in the big picture.

**Kate M. Gallagher** received her BA in English Literature and Creative Writing from Pomona College. She has studied poetry with Marvin Bell and Jorie Graham at the University of Iowa, and has participated in poetry readings in New York City and Westchester. She is also an editor, and teaches Creative Writing for children, adults, and the developmentally disabled at the Northern Westchester Center for the Arts and The Kids Short Story Connection in Greenburgh, NY.

**Ruth Handel** writes poetry to honor creation and to try to make sense of the world. Her poems have been published in several literary anthologies in print and on the web. She was a winner of 1996 Greenburgh, NY poetry contest and has presented readings of her poetry throughout the tri-state area. A political activist and retired professor of education, she has published academic papers and books throughout her professional career, including Building Family Literacy in an Urban Community (Teachers College Press, 1999). A New York native and long-time Westchester resident, Ruth has traveled many parts of the world, always with eager eyes and ears, pencil and notebook at the ready. She thinks the Poetry Caravan is one of the best ideas around.

**Adrienne Hernandez** is a poet and naturalist who lives in Hartsdale, New York. She is a wife, the mother of two children and a kindergarten teacher.

**Ina Marks** says English is her second language. She learned how to speak it very fast. She learned how to read very fast. She never learned how to spell. She carries her Webster's Dictionary from room to room when she has the urge to write a poem. Her friends like her poems.

**Dorothy Mate** is an 84-year old poet who has been writing rhymes for the past 25 years. She raised a family, worked in Real Estate and Travel. She has lived in Westchester for 54 years. She volunteers in the gift shop at Burke Rehabilitation. Her senior center is the focus of her energies where she is on the Executive Board. She has always volunteered for organizations she thought were worthwhile.

**Gertrude L. Moretti** majored in Philosophy at Smith college. After graduation she worked as a translator and researcher at the Nurnberg trial. Now married, with four children and nine grandchildren, she lives in Scarsdale, NY. She has been writing poetry since the 1960's. Most recently she has been reading Cavafy the Greek poet.

**Ralph Nazareth** is the Managing Editor of Yuganta Press and a professor of English at Nassau Community College.

**Laura Pacher North** has a BA in Comparative Literature from CCNY and an MA in Creative Writing from CCNY. She teaches at Lehman College. She writes poetry and personal narratives and her dream is to finish a novel about her father who has been dead more than half her life but who left behind a legacy of intrigue and sorrow. She is an animal rescuer and lives in Yonkers with seven cats and one dog.

**Leon Pantirer** was born in the Bronx in 1930 and has been writing poetry for the past twenty-five years. He has written several stories and many short stories that he believes are interesting for children, teenagers, and adults. His poetry has personal impact as well as humorous endings. They vary in the different and many miscellaneous subjects from articles in the NY Times, politics and sports, to the everyday events that suddenly pop up in life.

**Karen Rippstein** holds a BS degree in Writing as Therapy. She is currently data coordinator of Graduate Medical Education at New York Medical College and in training for certification as a poetry therapist with The National Association of Poetry Therapy. Her work has been published in *Personal Journaling Magazine* and the *NAPT Museletter.* Ms. Rippstein facilitates therapy/creative writing workshops with individuals and groups.

**Clare Rosenfield** writes poetry, essays, and stories, paints, meditates, and teaches people how to heal themselves in a holistic approach she calls Contact Healing ™. A Smith College graduate, former French teacher in Boston, Lagos, and Bangkok, and a social worker who received her M.S. from Columbia University, Clare integrates therapeutic approaches from East and West. She co-directs the Global Healing Foundation which shares creative ways to heal each other and our planet. Her poetry has appeared in numerous literary and therapeutic journals and anthologies. She has two books of poems and illustrations, *Roll On Great Earth*, and *The Call Of Mother Earth: How A Being Of Light Draws Forth Humanity's Response*. She and her husband have two married children and four grandchildren.

**Yselle Shapiro** is a performance poet who first got into print at age 14. Since then she has had many adventures. Most recently she read at the open mike on Division Street in Peekskill. She has been Jammin' for 25 years and nobody will believe the trouble she's been in. She grew up traveling, daughter of a diplomat, and sees herself as multicultural.

**Linda Simone's** poems have appeared in *Midnight Vigil*, *Westview*, *Potomac Review*, *Inkwell*, *Essential Love: Poems about mothers and fathers, daughters and sons* and other journals and anthologies. She served as poetry editor and managing editor for *Inkwell*, the literary journal of Manhattanville College.

**Frank Sisco** writes in various genres on a wide variety of topics. His poetry often deals with profound issues facing individuals in today's world. One example is a creative person's continual struggle to balance creative efforts with the need to work and provide for a family. Another example is the challenge of making relationships, especially with family members, as enriching as possible. Frank writes songs, with lyrics and music, of various styles including rock, pop, hip hop, and easy listening, often in the first person, recounting actual experiences. He also writes prose including an upcoming nonfiction book called "Dollars from Heaven - How to Put More God and More Money Into Your Life." Frank is a personal financial advisor to individuals and small businesses helping clients to shape and attain goals dealing with life and money issues.

**Patricia Smith** is four-time national individual champion of the poetry slam. In 1997, she tied with Jimmy Santiago Baca for the Taos Poetry Circus World Heavyweight Championship of Poetry. She is the author of three volumes of poetry— *Close to Death*, *Big Towns, Big Talk* and *Life According to Motown*. Smith's poems have been published in numerous literary journals and anthologies. She has won the prestigious Carl Sandburg Award, a literary award from the Illinois Arts Council and an honorary degree from the John Jay College of Criminal Justice. She is currently at work on two new poetry books, *Cracked Love* and *Teahouse of the Almighty*.

**Estelle Sudderth** loves reading poetry aloud to audiences. She is an active reader with *The Poetry Caravan*. She feels poems tell stories of adventure, lifestyles, love, sorrow, patriotism, war, religion, and all aspects of life.

**Margo Stever's** poems in this anthology are from her new collection of poems, *Raven's Rock*. She earned her postgraduate degrees from the Harvard Graduate School of Education (Ed.M, Reading and Human Development) and from Sarah Lawrence College (MFA, Poetry). Her poems and reviews have been published in numerous literary journals and poetry anthologies. Her chapbook, *Reading the Night Sky* (Introduction by Denise Levertov), was the winner of the 1996 Riverstone Poetry Chapbook Contest. Her manuscript, *Frozen Spring*, was the winner of the 2001 Mid-List Press First Series Award for Poetry. She is the founder and a current Board Member of The Hudson Valley Writers' Center and the founder and co-editor of the Slapering Hol Press.

**Gallia Taranto** is a visual artist who likes to write poetry. She says it is an immediate way of expressing her intimate or worldly thoughts into a certain "musical" structure.

She loves 'All Animals and all Beings of creation' and believes they are 'sent down here to teach us something.' Her dog has been a terrific Muse & inspiration for her writings and 'teaches me every day to live in the Present more than any meditation practice. He has also been my loyal companion through the darkness of the soul and cancer.'

**Pramila Venkateswaran,** author of *Thirtha*, a volume of poems published by Yuganta Press, has a doctorate from George Washington University and teaches English and women's studies and coordinates the Creative Writing Project at Nassau Community College, New York. A finalist for the Allen Ginsberg Poetry Award in 1999 and a recipient of a Hedgebrook residency in 2002 and a Norcroft residency in August 2003, she has published in Paterson Literary Review, Ariel: A Review of International English Literature, Atlanta Review, Prairie Schooner, Xanadu, Long Island Quarterly, Calyx: Journal of Art and Literature by Women, California Quarterly, and Nassau Review, among several other print and electronic journals. Recent anthologies, A Chorus for Peace and Writing the Lines of Our Hands, include her voice among poets from around the world.

**Charlotte Walsh** is a former dancer, choreographer and dance educator. Poetry has always been an important part of her life. She has completed two collections, *Echoes and Imprints* and *Poems from My Tree House*. She has taught poetry workshops for children and was awarded first prize in the 2002 Greenburgh Poetry Contest and third prize in 2003.